Loren Eiseley

LOREN EISELEY

A Modern Ishmael

PETER HEIDTMANN

Archon Books
1991

First published 1991 as an Archon Book,
an imprint of The Shoe String Press, Inc.,
Hamden, Connecticut 06514

Printed in the United States of America

The paper used in this publication meets the
minimum requirements of American National Standard
for Information Sciences—Permanence of Paper for
Printed Library Materials, ANSI Z39.48—1984 ♾

Library of Congress Cataloging-in-Publication Data

Heidtmann, Peter, 1937–
Loren Eiseley : a modern Ishmael / Peter Heidtmann
p. cm.
Includes bibliographical references and index.
1. Eiseley, Lorern C., 1907–1977—Biography.
2. Authors, American—20th century—Biography.
3. Anthropologists—United States—Biography.
4. Naturalists—United States—Biography.
I. Title
PS3555.178Z69 1991 301′.092—dc20 90-24756
ISBN 0-208-02293-7

The author is grateful to acknowledge the following permissions: The University of Pennsylvania Archives for the portrait photograph of Loren C. Eiseley; Alfred A. Knopf, Inc., for lines from *The Odyssey of Homer,* translated by Robert Fitzgerald, © 1961 by Robert Fitzgerald; The University of Nebraska Press for the following: "An Artist of Autumn" by Peter Heidtmann first appeared in an earlier form in *Prairie Schooner* 61 (Fall, 1987), pp. 46–56; lines from "The Wanderer" reprinted from *Poems from the Old English,* translated by Burton Raffel. Copyright © 1960, 1964 by the University of Nebraska Press. Lines from "The Second Coming" are reprinted with permission of Macmillan Publishing Company from *Collected Poems* of W. B. Yeats. Copyright 1924 by Macmillan Publishing Company, renewed 1952 by Bertha Georgie Yeats; lines from "The Mist on the Mountain" are reprinted with permission of Charles Scribner's Sons, an imprint of Macmillan Publishing Company, from *The Innocent Assassins* by Loren Eiseley. Copyright © 1973 by Loren Eiseley; lines from "A Hider's World" are reprinted with permission of Charles Scribner's Sons, an imprint of Macmillan Publishing Company, from *Another Kind of Autumn* by Loren Eiseley. Copyright © 1977 by the Estate of Loren Eiseley. Copyright © 1976 by Loren Eiseley.

For my mother and father

CONTENTS

ACKNOWLEDGMENTS

Short though it is, this book has had a long germination, beginning with a trip I made to Nebraska in the summer of 1981. At that time I had the good fortune to speak in Lincoln with Wilbur G. Gaffney and C. Bertrand Schultz, both of whom knew Loren Eiseley during their student days together at the university. The willingness of each to share some of his memories with me contributed significantly to my developing interest in the man. I am especially indebted to Professor Schultz for giving me a state map on which he had circled the sites where Eiseley worked as a member of the Morrill Expeditions during the early thirties. With that map as a guide, I was able to explore for myself the remote areas from which Eiseley derived his most memorable imagery when he later turned to the writing of essays.

I began more traditional research for the book in 1982 under the auspices of an Ohio University Faculty Fellowship, and accomplished later work with the help of a grant from the Ohio University Research Committee (1984–85). A significant amount of my research was conducted at the University of Pennsylvania Archives, where the extensive collection of Eiseley's papers is housed. I am grateful to the staff of the Archives, especially Maryellen C. Kaminsky and Curtis Ayres, for their unfailing courtesy and patience during my visits.

Two other people at Penn were also helpful to me along the way.

Dr. Ruben Reina of the anthropology department was generous with his time and reminiscences, while Trudy van Houten, then a graduate student in anthropology, first showed me the holdings of the Eiseley Library there.

Previously published studies of Eiseley's work have naturally contributed to my own understanding. Deserving of particular mention in this regard are the article by James Schwartz and the book by E. Fred Carlisle, both of which are listed in my bibliography. Henry Silver and Edgar Whan gave me more personal help by carefully reading and commenting on various portions of my original manuscript. In addition I owe special thanks to Gale Christianson. He not only read a complete draft of my work with a keen eye, but also generously allowed me to read several chapters in manuscript of his now-published biography of Eiseley.

Finally, I am grateful to my editor, James Thorpe III. His careful scrutiny of my manuscript impelled me to make many revisions that have strengthened the book, but naturally I alone am responsible for whatever weaknesses may remain.

ABBREVIATIONS

The following abbreviations of works by Loren Eiseley are used parenthetically throughout the text. (Page numbers are indicated by accompanying numerals.) Full bibliographic information on the works listed below is provided in the Bibliography.

AKA	*Another Kind of Autumn*
ANW	*All the Night Wings*
ASH	*All the Strange Hours*
EG	"The Enchanted Glass"
FT	*The Firmament of Time*
IA	*The Innocent Assassins*
IJ	*The Immense Journey*
IP	*The Invisible Pyramid*
NC	*The Night Country*
ST	*The Star Thrower*
UU	*The Unexpected Universe*

I

Approaching Eiseley's Essays

All sorrows can be borne if you put them
into a story or tell a story about them.
—Isak Dinesen

In "Nonfiction as the New American Literature" William Zinsser describes a shift in the habits of the reading public that took place after World War II. Prior to that time the bulk of the demand was for novels and short stories, but thereafter the appetite for works that dealt more directly with reality increased dramatically, so that by the early 1960s we had entered what he calls "a golden era of nonfiction." That era has by no means ended, and its vitality is partially reflected in a recently instituted annual collection called *The Best American Essays*.

As Robert Atwan, the general editor, declared when the series made its debut in 1986, "The modern American essay has adapted to the reading public's imperious demand for information, while retaining the personal, fluid, and speculative manner that has long characterized the form." Among the noteworthy postwar practitioners of this form, the earliest is Loren Eiseley, who began publishing in *Harper's* in 1947. And his enduring dedication to the art is made evident by the large number of essays he wrote during the remaining thirty years of his life. In fact, according to Annie Dillard, it is Eiseley who "restored the essay's place in imaginative literature" in this century.

A long-established critical tradition enables us to feel, usually, that we are on familiar ground when we attempt to come to grips with any given novelist or short story writer. The territory occupied by the essayist, however, has not been nearly so well staked out. That is because the form itself is so accepting and capacious that no area of human inquiry is alien to it. Nevertheless, with a writer of Eiseley's stature—one who has produced a significant body of work that has attracted a sizable readership—the effort required to suggest how he might best be read is well worth making.

In my undertaking of that task in this book, I devote little attention to the assessment of separate pieces. Some, naturally, are better than others. At his least effective Eiseley is given to the literary pose, to being self-indulgent and pretentious; yet he is also capable of writing prose of uncommon expressiveness and power. Generally I leave judgments of this sort concerning individual essays up to the individual reader. My main endeavor, instead, is to provide contexts and to identify themes that I believe will contribute to a better understanding and keener appreciation of Eiseley's accomplishment as a whole.

The first step we need to take toward arriving at that goal is to distinguish between the inner and the outer man. Richard Holmes, in discussing the hopeful assumption underlying the appeal of biography, has asserted that "[t]he public and the private life do, in the end, make sense of each other; and the one is meaningless without the other." Yet I do not find this to be true of Eiseley. On the contrary he is one of those writers who, like St. Augustine and H. D. Thoreau, demonstrates that the inner man alone can contain or reflect meanings deserving of a reader's sustained attention.

Consider for a moment the principal public facts of his life. Loren Corey Eiseley was born on September 3, 1907, in Lincoln, Nebraska, where he received most of his schooling. He first entered the university there in 1925, but did not graduate until 1933. In the fall of that year he enrolled in the graduate program in anthropology at the University of Pennsylvania and earned his doctorate in 1937. In August of 1938 he married Mabel Langdon. His lifelong academic career began in the department of sociology at the University of Kansas (1937–44). From there he moved to Oberlin College (1944–47), where he was appointed department chairman and professor of anthropology and sociology. Then, in the fall of 1947, he became chairman of the anthropology department at the University of Pennsylvania, and in 1948 he was also appointed curator of early man at the University Museum. In 1961, after a two-year term as provost of the university, he was named the first Benjamin Franklin Professor of Anthropology and the History of Science, a position he held until his death. He published thirteen books during his lifetime and four more have come out posthumously. On July 7, 1977, he died of cancer in Philadelphia.

Having this record before us, we can then consider how much bearing it has on the man who speaks to us through his books. In doing so I was reminded of a comment that Kate Chopin makes about her best-known fictional character: "At a very early period she had apprehended instinctively the dual life—that outward existence which conforms, the inward life which questions." This statement applies remarkably well to Eiseley. Outwardly, after emerging from obscure origins in Nebraska, he lived a very conventional adult life. Remaining quietly married to the same woman for forty years, he devoted himself to his long academic career, the last three decades of which were spent at the same prestigious institution. It is this figure who appears in many photographs: an easily recognizable professorial type with neatly combed silver hair, dark thick-rimmed glasses, conservative suit and tie. Yet in his published writings Eiseley tells us little about his outward existence. Instead the story we chiefly get, the one he felt driven to tell, is about the inward life which questions.

I use the word "story" purposefully here, because it seems to me that in his essays Eiseley is impelled primarily by the autobiographical impulse. My conviction that he is first and foremost a personal storyteller constitutes the basis for my approach to him in this book, an approach that needs to be explained (and perhaps defended) at the outset, since some readers are bound to object to it. Granted, they might say, *All the Strange Hours* is an autobiography of sorts. And, yes, our author did relate other personal experiences elsewhere, especially in *The Night Country*. But does this mean we should consider Loren Eiseley, the eminent man of science, a mere storyteller?

The question demands that the problem of how to categorize Eiseley be addressed. My purpose in doing so is to clarify the presuppositions that I believe are appropriate to bring to a reading of his essays. Eiseley was undeniably a scientist by training and a teacher of science by profession. It is also true that he wrote many articles for scholarly journals, especially early in his career, and that he produced *Darwin's Century*, an award-winning book in the history of science. But it is just as true that others would not have written books about him if he had done only those things. The fact is that Eiseley was first and foremost an artist, a writer in the imaginative sense of the term, one who had the ability to use words in a way that readers find both moving and memorable.

It is therefore misleading to think of Eiseley chiefly as a scientist or academician. For one thing, except in his early professional articles, he does not address himself to the scientific community, but to the reading public at large. Nor is he chiefly concerned to make scientific ideas accessible to the layman; he is not a popularizer of science in the expert manner of a Jacob Bronowski or a Stephen Jay Gould. Instead, while he has enormous respect for the external physical world, he approaches it in an avowedly subjective manner. "[H]ere is a bit of my personal universe," he says in his very first book, "a universe traversed in a long and uncompleted journey" (*IJ*,13). And the record of that journey is continued in most of his subsequent books, works in which he moves still further away from scientific objectivity and, in many places, even from scientific concerns.

The principal medium that Eiseley uses for his mental prowlings is the essay, a highly malleable genre, which at its best subtly reflects the personality of the essayist. Its primary source of interest, as Eiseley recognizes in alluding to Montaigne and Emerson, is "the self and its minute adventures" (*ASH*,183). Contained in the last of his books to be published before his death, this formulation—*the adventures of the self*—gives us the key to his main preoccupation as a writer.

Yet this expression of his concern is anticipated in a comment Eiseley made two decades earlier, not long before the publication of his first book, *The Immense Journey*. In a letter of December 1956, addressed to his editor, he refers to the name he has proposed for the work, saying, "I feel a little wistful about my late discovery of what I think is a wonderful title that should have been applied to an autobiography which remains unwritten." And when he sought a Guggenheim Fellowship in 1962, he still had that autobiography in mind, because a reading of the application shows that his intention was to explore material he did not actually get around to until more than ten years later in *All the Strange Hours* (1975). Not yet ready to handle some of the painful experiences from childhood and youth that appear there, he turned instead to other projects, including *The Unexpected Universe* (1969) and *The Night Country* (1971), both of which nevertheless contain essays of great personal significance.

Anyone interested in tracking down Eiseley's many works in a library, however, is confronted with an unusual phenomenon. As James M. Schwartz has pointed out, only the volumes of poems are classified by the Library of Congress system under "P" (for literature). Otherwise, one discovers, the rest of his books are catalogued under "B" (for philosophy and religion), "C" (for history), "G" (for geography and anthropology), "Q" (for science), and "R" (for medicine). An advantage of the autobiographical approach to be developed here is that it enables us to view this bewildering variety from a consistent perspective. Moreover, it helps us to understand Eiseley's essays within a significant context of American letters. Alfred Kazin has observed that several of our major writers—Emerson, Thoreau, Whitman, and Henry Adams, for example—"tend to project the world as a picture of themselves even when they are not writing directly about themselves." As the pages to come will show, Eiseley is clearly an author of this sort as well.

Thus we do not misrepresent Eiseley by considering him an autobiographical artist. On the contrary, since he devoted so much attention to the writing of personal narratives, we are obliged to acknowledge that he considered it an important endeavor. It is not important, to be sure, in the same way that professional achievements are, but our estimation of Eiseley's work should not be governed by our knowledge of his external academic career. If we shift our critical gaze away from the scientific subject matter of many of his essays and focus instead on his individual manner of *presenting* his material, then we find ourselves led to a different way of understanding his accomplishment. In order for this to happen we must allow ourselves to be guided by the voice within the essays—the lyrical, often melancholy, sometimes forlorn voice that projects his inward self.

Anyone disposed to modify the word "storyteller" with the word "mere" misapprehends the value of an ancient art. Such misapprehension, as all his readers know, could never be attributed to Eiseley. In the remainder of this chapter my intention is to discuss the importance of storytelling, especially in its modern autobiographical manifestations, and to provide an initial indication of Eiseley's place within that context.

Loren Eiseley would surely have agreed with Laurens van der Post's account of what he learned from the African Bushman. In part he says,

> The supreme expression of his spirit was in his stories. He was a wonderful story-teller. The story was his most sacred possession. These people knew what we do not: that without a story you have not got a nation, or a culture, or a civilization. Without a story of your own to live you haven't got a life of your own.

Yet, as Eiseley also knew, we were not always ignorant in these matters, for some of the monuments of our literature testify to the importance of stories and storytelling.

Homer, for instance, presents us with a revealing scene in Book VIII of *The Odyssey*. It takes place at the court of King Alkinoös where Odysseus, although not yet known by name to his host, has arrived near the end of his long wanderings. At a banquet held in honor of the visitor, Demodokos, the blind bard, sings tales of the heroes of the Trojan War. Even though we are to assume that everyone present has often heard of the exploits of these men before, the entire company listens attentively, and Odysseus weeps in his cloak. Later, before asking the harpist to sing again, this time about the illustrious wooden horse, he enthusiastically praises Demodokos, saying (in the Fitzgerald translation),

> All men owe honor to the poets—honor
> and awe, for they are dearest to the Muse
> who puts upon their lips the ways of life.

Likewise the *Beowulf*-poet describes festive occasions when the singer of tales entertains others with stories known among all the Germanic peoples—stories of creation, for example, or of the adventures of dragonslayers from former days. Especially significant is the scene that takes place the morning after Beowulf's fight with Grendel, when many warriors follow the track of the wounded monster to the banks of the dark pool that is his dwelling place. Satisfied to find the turbulent water roiling with blood, they ride jubilantly back to Hrothgar's hall, while a skillful bard who remembered many of the old stories relates for the first time an account of the struggle, putting into well-linked words a tale of the youthful victor who now shows promise of becoming a figure of genuine heroic stature.

Although the societies of Homer and the *Beowulf*-poet had advanced beyond the Stone Age culture represented by the Bushmen, both were nevertheless preliterate. What the two poets had in common was access to a fund of traditional tales, which they sometimes depict as being told by storytellers who are characters within their epics. These characters are always noteworthy because they are the repositories of their people's history, of the stories that bind them together and give them their identity as a people. Thus, while Odysseus and Beowulf have their own legendary biographies, these life-stories do not belong to them alone. Instead, because of the skill and saving memory of many oral poets, their stories and those of countless others become treasured communal possessions, shared by all the people generation after generation.

The communities reflected in *The Odyssey* and in *Beowulf* were small in scale and homogeneous, still analogous to that of the

Bushmen who lived in groups of thirty or forty. But it was not literacy or an increase in size and complexity alone that brought about our present disconnection from a common fund of stories. With the advent of Christianity, after all, an overarching myth evolved in Europe that bound many diverse peoples together for centuries. Yet there can be no doubt that, at least since the Reformation, Western culture has become increasingly characterized by a sense of dislocation and fragmentation. "'Tis all in pieces, all coherence gone," wrote John Donne in "The First Anniversary" early in the seventeenth century. And three hundred years later the sentiment was echoed by W. B. Yeats in the opening lines of "The Second Coming":

> Turning and turning in the widening gyre
> The falcon cannot hear the falconer;
> Things fall apart; the centre cannot hold. . . .

In reading such pronouncements we must of course make allowances for nostalgia, for the common human tendency to idealize the past and denigrate the present. As E. M. Forster has written, "Order . . . is an internal stability, a vital harmony, and in the social and political category it has never existed except for the convenience of historians." Nevertheless, the disorder of modern life is different in degree from that in the past because of the ever-accelerating rate at which change has taken place since the Industrial Revolution. Charles Lindbergh, for example, was hailed as a hero for flying across the Atlantic in 1927, yet a mere forty years later, during Lindbergh's own lifetime, advances in science and technology enabled astronauts to rocket to the moon. Change has become a juggernaut that threatens to crush all hope of order. As Forster asks, "How can man get into harmony with his surroundings when he is constantly altering them?"

Yet the "internal stability" and "vital harmony" he also mentions has always been present in the realm of art, and still can be—indeed, still must be—sought there. Despite the disintegration of our communal sense, despite our sense of isolation as manifested in our having been cut off from participation in the shared stories once so vital to our ancestors, the need for stories remains. Human beings are meaning-seekers, which is to say that we long to give form to our lives, to make connections by fitting apparently disparate events into larger, mind-satisfying configurations. Just as Beowulf's individual struggle with Grendel could acquire significance only by being recounted within a broader context of heroic endeavor, so we feel the need to put the experiences of our own more ordinary lives into some framework that will invest them with meaning.

Granted, we have a more difficult job. To begin with we are not all skillful storytellers as were the oral poets among our preliterate forebears. Nor can we look to anyone, blessed by the Muse, who can tell us "the ways of life." Nowadays there is no common path. A major problem that we have is connecting our lives with something beyond the individual self, because it is only by doing so that we can hope to find the meaning we seek. Lacking direct access to a previously established story-hoard or mythology, we search for ways of providing our own larger contexts of signification, of creating our own individual myths.

It is now widely recognized by students of autobiography that all our memorable life-writers have in fact accomplished this feat. Perhaps we can better understand their achievement if we consider an analogy between the autobiographer and the sculptor. The latter works with an undifferentiated mass of material, a solid block of marble, and out of it, if he has the genius, creates a "David." Michaelangelo was able to produce this magnificent figure through a process of discarding, of chiseling away. "David," we might say, was just one of the forms latent in the mass of marble, yet the sculptor made it visible by what he removed from the original block. Similarly the autobiographer, working with an incoherent mass of material—his life as actually lived—creates a memorable human image largely through what he leaves out. Of course there is the need to arrange what remains, but for the sake of this analogy we can see that the autobiographer, like the sculptor, practices an art of exclusion.

Two contemporary memoirists, William Zinsser and Russell Baker, testify to the truth of this point. The first declares that the autobiographical writer inevitably becomes "the editor of his own life," cutting and pruning an unwieldy story to "give it a narrative shape." Baker is even more emphatic. After contrasting the biographer and the autobiographer, claiming that the former never knows enough while the latter always knows too much, he concludes: "So when you're writing about yourself, the problem is what to leave out."

All this purposeful omission of material necessarily makes the written account of the memoirist's experience markedly different from his or her actual experience. The object of my concern in this study is the first of these—the life text rather than the lived life—and I agree with Roy Pascal's general view of its potential effect upon the reader. He asserts that the value and truth of autobiographical writing arises from "*the monolithic impact* of a personality that out of its own and the world's infinitude forms round itself, through composition and style, a homogeneous entity both in the sense that it operates consistently on the world and in the sense that it creates a consistent series of mental images out of its encounter with the world" (my emphasis). No one could actually live in such an artful fashion, yet in his writing the autobiographer is able to overcome the diffuseness and routine banality of daily life largely by exercising his prerogative to exclude.

This becomes especially apparent in regard to autobiographical writers when we consider their work in the light of what a biographer would be obliged to include. Although Russell Baker may be right to say that a biographer can never know enough, certainly his aim is to uncover as much information as possible about his subject. This task has now been ably performed for Loren Eiseley by Gale Christianson, who has given us as complete an account of the man's life as we are ever likely to get.

Completeness of biographical detail, however, is something we must not expect to find in Eiseley's own work. Nor do we find it in the memorable autobiographical writings of some of his American predecessors. A brief consideration of two of them, Henry Adams and Henry David Thoreau, will help provide some perspective on the nature of Eiseley's endeavor.

Adams said that he used *The Confessions of St. Augustine* as a literary model in writing *The Education of Henry Adams*. What he especially admired about Augustine was his way of presenting "a story with an end and object, not for the sake of the object, but for the form, like a romance." Struggling mightily with the problem of form himself, Adams succeeded in making his own adaptation of the romance by establishing his protagonist as a peculiarly modern quester or pilgrim. The author sets his namesake out on the road of life armed with the traditionally sanctioned verities of his time and class, but these weapons prove to be hopelessly weak and archaic in the face of the challenges presented by nineteenth-century life. Consequently a pattern is established wherein the young seeker after meaning is put to repeated tests that fail to yield the desired results. This pattern of trial and defeat provides the basic criterion for Adams to determine what episodes to include in the book. Anything that doesn't fit the pattern can be excluded on the grounds of being irrelevant to the story he has decided to tell. The most noteworthy example of this is his omission of two decades of his life entirely, the years from 1871 to 1892, which were extraordinary in terms of his productivity as a writer, and during which time he both married and suffered the catastrophe of his wife's suicide.

The reader who wants to know more concerning Henry Adams, to find out about his many accomplishments, for instance, or about the domestic side of his life, must turn to other books, especially Ernest Samuels's three-volume biography. Yet it is only in the *Education* that we get the story the author wanted to tell, the story of the mythic Adams who even in his late sixties, tired though he was, would not think of giving up the struggle despite his sense of failure. "As long as he could whisper," we are told, "he would go on as he had begun, bluntly refusing to meet his creator with the admission that the creation had taught him nothing except that the square of the hypothenuse of a right-angled triangle might for convenience be taken as equal to something else." This spirit of dogged, sardonically clear-headed determination animates the whole work and contributes to the development of a figure of heroic stature. By the end of the book Adams emerges as a man cut in the mold of

Tennyson's Ulysses, who, tireless in his search for knowledge, remains "strong in will / To strive, to seek, to find, but not to yield."

Turning to Thoreau, we find that he presents a still more extreme example of what I am suggesting here about artful autobiographical writing. Extreme because, to begin with, *Walden* is scarcely an autobiography at all in the traditional sense. Instead of telling the story of many consecutive years of his past, Thoreau tells us about only one self-contained segment of his life. In acutality it occupied a period of two years and two months, but Thoreau makes it seem even shorter by compressing it into the span of just one year. *Walden* is an extreme case in a still more significant sense, however, because of the extent of its exclusions.

The surface story is easily summarized. Borrowing an ax in March of 1845, and going down to the woods by Walden Pond, Thoreau began to build a cabin that he moved into on July 4. He did so, he says, because he wished to confront only the essential facts of life in order to discover what it had to teach. While at the pond he lived in Spartan style, working as needed in his beanfield, but mostly he was concerned to recount his thoughts and observations as the seasons of the year progressed from one spring to the next. Then he left the woods to become a sojourner in civilized life again because he had other lives to live.

Only by consulting other sources can we learn more about the circumstances of this extended episode in Thoreau's life. A reading of Walter Harding's *The Days of Henry Thoreau*, for instance, reveals that he was not nearly so remote and solitary during this period as *Walden* suggests. His cabin was only two miles from the center of Concord, the Thoreau family house was even less than that, and the much-traveled Concord-Lincoln Road could be seen from where he stayed. In addition he often had visitors at the pond, ranging from such men as Emerson, Hawthorne, and Bronson Alcott, to parties of children from the village. Furthermore Henry's mother and sisters made a trip to see him every Saturday with offerings of food. And on his own almost daily visits home Thoreau was un-Spartan enough to make frequent raids on his mother's well-stocked cookie jar.

But what do these details matter in regard to the book we all know? *Walden*, to an even greater degree than Adams's *Education*, illustrates Georges Gusdorf's point that insofar as an autobiography is a work of art, it shows us not "the individual seen from the outside in his visible actions, but the person in his inner privacy, not as he was, not as he is, but as he believes himself to be and to have been." The real story of *Walden* is an inner one, in which external biographical detail plays scarcely any part, with Thoreau himself cast in the role of the solitary hero. He acknowledges the difficulty of exploring "the private sea, the Atlantic and Pacific Ocean of one's being alone," but he is nevertheless a strong advocate of the undertaking. A clear sign of his own success at the task is that his book is now seen not simply as one man's idiosyncratic account of his experience but as the expression of an American myth of self-reliance and self-renewal. "For a biographer who seeks all the little facts and tries to establish all the tidy little truths," Leon Edel has written, "*Walden* holds a high cautionary lesson. A legend can be more powerful than the truth—indeed, in the end it can become the truth."

This discussion inevitably raises the question of the relationship between autobiography and fiction. It is a knotty topic, one much debated nowadays among theorists of autobiography. While it would not serve our purpose to take an excursion into the field of theory, two points are worth making here. The first is that "reality" can never be duplicated in words, whether they are used by a scientist, a historian, or anyone else. The best we can do through language is construct a verison of what appears to be true or real to us. Russell Baker realized this when, after finishing all the research plus a 400-page draft of the book that became *Growing Up*, he announced to his wife: "I am now going upstairs to invent the story of my life." His declaration introduces my second point, which is that the actual practice of writers we call autobiographical contradicts our ordinary notion of the factuality of nonfiction. Few would claim that *The Education of Henry Adams* and *Walden* are novels, yet, as we have seen, they do not simply present chronological, inclusive accounts of their authors' pasts. That is because autobiographical writers, in order to make sense out of their experience, in order to discover the kind of truth that only coherence can bring, must tell stories about themselves. And once we recognize that this is so, then we are obliged to accept as a given the blurring of the borderline between fiction and nonfiction in autobiographical writing.

Like Adams, and especially like Thoreau, a man with whom he felt a great affinity, Loren Eiseley created a mythic image of himself in his writings. Unlike them, however, he did not do so within the confines of a single book. Two years before he died he published *All the Strange Hours*, which is the only one of his many works that can be labeled an autobiography. Yet Eiseley himself acknowledged that all his previous personal essays constitute a kind of "continuing autobiography." One consequence of this is that some material that would ordinarily have been included in *All the Strange Hours* was omitted because he had already dealt with it elsewhere. Second, Eiseley's preference for the essay form means that we need to look for him in many places across a span of thirty years. In this sense Eiseley is comparable to Montaigne, another elusive figure whose track must be followed through a myriad of separate pieces. Because innumerable readers have done just that during the last four centuries, an image of Montaigne, the presiding presence of his collected essays, has come into focus. In a similar way I want to concentrate on clarifying the features of the figure who emerges in the pages of Eiseley's books.

So ingrained was Eiseley's habitual method of composition that even *All the Strange Hours* is not, by his own admission, "a consistent narrative" (*ASH*, 234). This point is important because the choice of the essay form has significant implications in regard to our expectations as readers. Since the personal essay does not permit extended narration, it reflects Eiseley's temperamental unsuitability for autobiographical writing of the traditional historical sort, such as that undertaken by Benjamin Franklin. Autobiography in this mode, as William C. Spengemann has pointed out, explains "the relation of an individual life to the shared beliefs of its stipulated audience." The writer's method is to select events from his past and arrange them into a retrospective narrative pattern that "simultaneously illustrates his opinions and shows how he came to hold them." But the collapse of shared beliefs in the modern world has made this kind of life-writing increasingly difficult. Even when it is attempted by one as accomplished as Bertrand Russell, according to Michael G. Cooke, the result is not so much an autobiography as "a chronicle bedevilled by personality."

More relevant to Eiseley's brand of self-exploration is the kind of nonhistorical autobiography that has come into prominence since the days when Rousseau and Wordsworth were at work. Acutely aware of a disjunction between themselves and their society, these two writers and their inheritors are less concerned with consensual values than they are with personal, inner truth. Consequently they "shun the foregone conclusions of retrospectively selected and arranged self-biography to prospect for the self through the organic formulations of philosophic inquiry and poetic expression." As an autobiographical essayist, Eiseley clearly belongs to this essentially romantic tradition.

The very nature of his exclusions suggests as much. Consider an example that surfaced in a conversation I had with Wilbur G. Gaffney, one of Eiseley's best friends during their college days. Professor Gaffney, then a retired member of the English faculty at the University of Nebraska and now deceased, fondly recalled the day-long hikes that he and Loren often took across the high prairie west of Lincoln. What bound them together was not only their love of the outdoors but also their love of poetry, many lines of which they had learned by heart and declaimed to the earth and sky as they walked. But the light went out of the old man's eyes when he further recalled that Eiseley makes no mention of him and those heady days of their youth in *All the Strange Hours*. "It's as if I didn't exist," he said.

An exclusion of this sort, I came to understand later, is typical of Eiseley and illustrates a basic difference between his life as lived and as reconstructed in his writings. That difference depends on our recognizing the inherent doubleness of human experience, as previously described in the quotation from Kate Chopin. Eiseley himself alluded to this duality when, while discussing his childhood in an interview, he distinguished between the public life of the boy in the streets and the withdrawn life of that same boy at home. Rather than diminish as he grew older, the rift between these two aspects of his experience became, if anything, more pronounced. More will be made of this in the next chapter, but for now it needs to be emphasized that Eiseley shows little interest in the social or public dimensions of life in his work. He is almost as mute as Henry Adams about his marriage, for instance, mentioning his wife of forty years only incidentally in *All the Strange Hours*. Neither does he provide a satisfying account of his career. Bearing in mind a comment W. H. Auden once made about every man being "both a citizen and a pilgrim," we are bound to recognize that citizen Eiseley plays a remarkably minor role in his books. The focus instead is on his private, solitary experience—on the pilgrim side of his nature—because of his preoccupation with inner truth.

Prompted at least partly by this concern, Eiseley also does not hesitate to alter his experiences in writing about them. He openly admits as much in regard to "The Relic Men," for instance, an essay in *The Night Country*. Although the book came out in 1971, part of this essay was originally published twenty-three years earlier in *Harper's* under the title of "Buzby's Petrified Woman." At the time (1948) Eiseley provided a note to accompany the piece in which he indicated that while it was based on an actual incident from his bone-hunting days, it had become a kind of short story in his retelling. He admits, in other words, to tampering with autobiographical fact for the sake of artistic effect.

A more complex example concerns the episode of the freeing of the hawks as described in "The Bird and the Machine," one of the essays in *The Immense Journey*. The actual event took place in May of 1932, and is recounted by Gale Christianson on the authority of C. Bertrand Schultz, Eiseley's most enduring friend from their years together at the University of Nebraska. At the time they had arrived at an excavation site on a ranch in the western part of the state. During their first night Schultz and his wife discovered that the abandoned cabin where they were told they could stay was already occupied by a pair of nesting sparrow hawks. The male soon left through a hole in the roof, but the female, feeling her nest threatened, stayed to pester the couple throughout the night. Eiseley, who had slept in a tent nearby, learned of the problem in the morning. With Schultz's help he cornered the female, got her into a gunny sack, and, after repairing the hole in the roof, released her outside.

Eiseley's rendition of the episode, as every reader of the published essay knows, is strikingly different. In it he presents himself as entering the cabin alone at night because part of his job was to help capture some live birds for a zoo. When he reached his arm over a shelf near the eaves, a male hawk sank his beak into his captor's thumb, thereby allowing the female to fly free through the dilapidated roof. "The little fellow had saved his mate by diverting me and that was that," Eiseley says (*IJ*,189). In the morning, instead of taking the male to the waiting trucks, he scanned the sky, hoping that the female had not left for good. Although he saw no sign of her, he furtively released the hawk, whereupon he heard a heart-wrenching cry, uttered by the female, who came diving out of the blinding sun to meet her mate. Eiseley then writes this memorable passage:

> I saw them both now. He was rising fast to meet her. They met in a great soaring gyre that turned to a whirling circle and a dance of wings. Once more, just once, their two voices, joined in a harsh wild medley of question and response, struck and echoed against the pinnacles of the valley. Then they were gone forever somewhere into those upper regions beyond the eyes of men (*IJ*,192).

How are we to account for the disparity between the actual event and Eiseley's presentation of it? An interesting possibility is suggested by additional information contained in Professor Christianson's biography. He informs us that the previous summer (1931) Mabel Langdon left Lincoln for the purpose of gaining some perspective on the uncertain years-long relationship she had already had with Loren. During her absence, feeling free to date as he pleased, Eiseley fell in love with a woman named Helen. The feeling was mutual and they wanted to marry, but then he received a letter from Mabel declaring her intention of returning to Lincoln with a renewed commitment to him. Emotionally torn, Eiseley was unable to make a firm choice between the woman he now loved and the woman toward whom he felt a sense of loyalty and obligation. Consequently, and for various reasons, Helen herself decided to step aside before Mabel's return. This was a painful decision for her, and it left Eiseley "haunted by the failure of their summer romance and his lack of personal resolve."

A psychological connection between this experience and the story about the two birds in *The Immense Journey* seems plausible, for as Eiseley acknowledges in introducing the episode, "It is a funny thing what the brain will do with memories" (*IJ*,179). In this case the male hawk defends his mate and himself from outside interference, taking the sort of resolute action that Eiseley admires but of which he was incapable in regard to Helen. In addition he brings about an ecstatically happy ending for the story of the hawks, the sort of ending that had eluded him in his actual life. This interpretation is necessarily conjectural, and I do not mean to imply that Eiseley was consciously atoning for his failed love affair by writing as he did about the two birds. At the same time we cannot simply dismiss this possible source for the story; surely there have been stranger transformations of life into art.

Eiseley explains his own understanding of such transformations in the description he has left us of a writer's mind. He compares it to an "unseen artist's loft" and elaborates on the analogy in this way:

> There are pictures that hang askew, pictures with outlines barely chalked in, pictures torn, pictures the artist has striven unsuccessfully to erase, pictures that only emerge and glow in a certain light. They have all been teleported, stolen, as it were, out of time. They represent no longer the sequential flow of ordinary memory. . . . The writer sees back to these transports alone, bare, perhaps few in number, but endowed with symbolic life. He cannot obliterate them. He can only drag them about, magnify or reduce them as his artistic sense dictates, or juxtapose them in order to enhance a pattern (*ASH*,156).

This passage further clarifies Eiseley's romantic heritage. For one thing the emphasis on symbolic, nonsequential images connects him with Rousseau's moments of heightened feeling as well as with Wordsworth's spots of time. In addition his avowed willingness to manipulate these images for artistic purposes shows that, like Thoreau, he does not feel himself bound by a strict sense of fact. A writer who works in the manner thus described is especially qualified to be the kind of "philosophico-poetic" autobiographer heralded by Carlyle in *Sartor Resartus*.

And this, indeed, is the kind of essayist Eiseley was. He would readily have agreed with Barrett J. Mandel that autobiographical writing is one of the strategies we humans have developed to counter our awareness that life has a way of not living up to our expectations. It is a means "to make life matter." Eiseley suggests as much in this passage from one of his letters: "[T]o a discerning eye," he wrote, "I am there in my books, more articulate and less limping than I would be in any personal interview." The context shows that he was chiefly concerned with self-protection when he made the comment, yet it hints at something more. The implication is that the essential truth about himself—to be distinguished from the objective truth with which biographers are primarily concerned—is to be found only in his work. Only there, as in the books by Henry Adams and Henry Thoreau, does he emerge as the protagonist of his own mythic story, in which, if he has been sufficiently skillful and fortunate, he too may acquire in the end something of the stature and solidity of Michaelangelo's "David." It is this figure, the Eiseley persona rather than the historical personage, with whom we will be concerned in the chapters to follow.

II

Memory and Myth

> I would so state facts that they shall be
> significant, shall be myths or mythologic.
> —H. D. Thoreau

By my words you shall know me. This is the implicit pledge that every autobiographer makes to his reader, and Loren Eiseley is no exception. He would have given his full assent to Avrom Fleischman's view that "an autobiography does not represent or repeat a life but instead brings it into existence. 'Life' means nothing in the individual (as distinct from the biological) realm until it is told in life stories." In a way the autobiographer performs on an individual scale the task that the mythological Marduk undertook for the world at large. Just as the Babylonian god threw his net over Tiamet, the principal dragon of chaos, and cut her into pieces to establish the order of the universe, so the life-writer's words constitute "a network of intelligibility" that he casts over his experience to create a meaningful personal world.

Thus Eiseley's experience, like that of Adams and Thoreau, acquires a satisfying form as a result of being embodied in the story of his life that is presented in his books. That story has its beginnings in his strange childhood, develops further during his troubled youth, and finds its fulfillment in his brooding maturity. The focus of this chapter is on the first two of these three stages.

In his personal essays Eiseley places a great deal of emphasis on his early years, which is another sign of his romantic heritage. Nor is this simply a matter of having been born shortly after the end of the nineteenth century, as the example of George Kennan well illustrates. Three years older than Eiseley, Kennan produced an account of his past that *begins* when he was twenty-one. He justifies this approach by comparing the movement through life to a journey through a dark wood with the aid of a lantern. As he puts it, "A bit of the path ahead is illuminated and a bit of the path behind. But the darkness follows hard on one's footsteps, and envelopes our trail as one proceeds." Consequently, he declares, "We are, toward the end of our lives, such different people, so far removed from the childhood figures with whom our identity links us, that the bond to those figures, like that of nations to their obscure prehistoric origins, is almost irrelevant." Nothing could be further removed from the outlook of Eiseley, who would surely have agreed with Wordsworth's famous dictum about the child being father of the man.

Memory, of course, plays a vital role in Eiseley's presentation of his childhood and youth. Without that essential faculty he could not have dealt with his past at all. Yet we need to remember that it is not the past itself that we encounter in his essays. What we find instead are images of the past as they existed in the mind of the adult writer. Thus we must pay attention not only to the content of the material unlocked by the key of memory but also to the manner of its presentation. Doing so will enable us to move toward an understanding of Eiseley's personal brand of myth-making.

If, in old age, time can be likened to "the splintered glass of a mirror" (*ASH*, 6), then the autobiographer's task becomes one of piecing together some of the images reflected in the fragments. Eiseley does this for his childhood and youth by telling many stories that are presented as memories of those early years. Readers of *The Night Country* and *All the Strange Hours* will be acquainted with the narratives summarized below, but they need to be assembled in one place for their cumulative effect to be felt.

Near the beginning of "The Mind as Nature," contained in *The Night Country*, Eiseley makes some statements that provide a framework for his perceptions of his early family situation. There we are told that the Eiseleys were social outcasts of a sort, living in a house where the parlor was always kept shuttered against the light because they never had visitors and no minister ever came to call. "We were not bad people nor did we belong to a racial minority," he writes. "We were simply shunned as unimportant and odd" (*NC*,197).

The oddity was largely attributable to Eiseley's mother, the person in his life about whom he has more to say than any other. Daisy Corey Eiseley was deaf, having lost her hearing in childhood, and young Loren therefore often found himself in a house where "dead silence was broken only by the harsh discordant jangling of a voice that could not hear itself" (*NC*, 197). Although he admits that Daisy loved him in a "tigerish silent way" (*ASH*, 31), he describes her as being "paranoid, neurotic, and unstable," a woman whom he never saw weep and who had a talent for making others suffer (*ASH*, 24). In contemplating the cause of his mother's condition, Eiseley wonders about the influence of certain forebears, the Shepards, who were reputed to be mad, but he judges that her deafness itself was probably the main reason for her imbalance. No matter what the cause, however, there was no possibility of feeling close to her.

In one passage he recalls falling through the ice of a pond on which he had been skating alone. He was able to save himself, but the point of the episode is that there was no chance of his finding comfort at home. He could not even reveal what had happened because he knew that only hysterical admonitions would follow, and he might well be kept inside. "Slowly my inner life was continuing to adjust to this fact," he says. "I had to rely on silence. It was like creeping away from death out of an ice hole an inch at a time. You did it alone" (*ASH*, 171).

In another, more vividly detailed episode, he remembers an occasion when his mother's restless, possessive behavior passed out of bounds. He was ten years old and playing with some other boys in a pasture, when she came to order him home. Feeling a sense of humiliation in front of the others, he forsook a promise he had made earlier to his father, a promise not to cross his mother because she was not responsible. Instead of obeying her violent gesticulations he ran away, "with the witch, her hair flying, her clothing disarrayed, stumbling after" (*ASH*, 34). All he could think of at that moment was escape, which, when temporarily achieved, was followed by an overwhelming sense of shame.

In this disturbing scene Daisy is portrayed as an alien creature with distorted features, one who repels rather than attracts. In fact Eiseley almost never speaks of her with sympathy. Years after her death, it is true, he claims to be no longer embittered. Standing above her grave, he murmurs to himself, trying to tell her that all the suffering they endured "was for nothing" (*ASH*, 25). Yet it is hard to understand what this means. A life-long anguished relationship cannot be dismissed with a few belated words, as is made painfully clear in the account of Daisy's funeral. At first Eiseley is unwilling to view the body because he "wished to look no more upon that rouged and ravaged face," feeling "empty of gratitude to this woman who had given [him] life and at the same time had well-nigh destroyed it" (*ASH*, 230). He then relents but only for a moment, convinced that, as always, she had finally had her way, drawing him to her side one last time against his will. Furthermore, in the graveyard scene referred to above, he acknowledges that neither of them would rest even in death if he were to be buried near her. Despite his disclaimer, then, Eiseley's bitterness toward Daisy did not die with her; at least some of it remained with him to the end of his days.

Just the opposite is true of Eiseley's response to his father. He tells us that Clyde was "a mild-mannered man with a deep faith in the essential goodness of the working class" to which he belonged (*ASH*, 11). Although he was a failure in a worldly sense, he was an admirable man. He "bore the asperities of my afflicted mother with dignity and restraint," Eiseley writes, and in general was "kind and thoughtful with an innate courtesy that no school in that rough land had taught him" (*NC*, 198, 199). Of course desertion, "the poor man's divorce," was always open to him, but he rejected this easy way out (*ASH*, 32). Instead, despite the urgings of his closest relatives, he stayed for the sake of his son. For this Eiseley was forever grateful, since he would have been left "inarticulate" if his father had fled (*NC*, 199).

Forty years after his father's death he still fondly remembered the man who had once been an itinerant actor and occasionally recited passages aloud from Shakespeare. Declaimed in a beautifully resonant voice, lines such as "Give me my Robe, put on my Crowne; I have / Immortall longings in me," caused shivers to run up young Loren's back (*NC*, 198). Eiseley's feeling toward his father is perhaps most memorably revealed, however, in a passage concerning a cottonwood tree. He explains that the two of them had planted a sapling in the yard of a house where he once lived as a boy, and that when he was in his sixties he made a point of returning to the site. To his disappointment he discovered that the tree had not survived, but throughout the years, he tells us, "it had been growing in my mind, a huge tree that somehow stood for my father and the love I bore him" (*NC*, 235).

That love persevered in the face of both absence and unhappiness in childhood. Because his father worked long hours away from home, Loren would usually be left alone with his mother. Yet when both parents were present there was often marital strife. Eiseley mentions their endless pacing and midnight arguments, recalling that once at age four "I climbed from bed and seized their hands, pleading wordlessly for sleep, for peace, peace" (*ASH*, 26). Never did he learn what brought their marriage about—a middle-aged one for his father—nor "by what fantastic chance I had come to exist at all" (*NC*, 197).

Through the vividness of the images contained in these recollections, Eiseley conveys a powerful impression of the influence that his earliest years apparently had upon him. "Terror, anxiety, ostracism, shame; I did not understand the words," he writes. "I learned only the feelings they represent" (*ASH*, 26). The suggestion implicit in the foregoing description of the Eiseley household is that it almost inevitably produced "a curiously deprived and solitary child" (*NC*, 199). Certainly, as this collection of memories makes clear, Eiseley saw his boyhood home as neither a refuge nor a warm nourisher of the spirit. Instead, despite the positive presence of his father, it was a place from which to escape. Eiseley did just that in the course of growing up, but his first tentative forays into a larger world held out no promise of comfort.

In his earliest remembrance of being with other children, he tells of joining a group of older boys from a different part of town who went to play by a pool in a sandstone basin. There they found a huge turtle that the others pounded to death with stones while Eiseley, never having seen death before, looked on in horror. When they were finished with the turtle, the older boys next turned against their younger companion, hitting him directly as well as pelting him with stones, before finally driving him away in the dark. By following the spots of light shed by street lamps along the unfamiliar road, Eiseley found his frightened way home alone (*NC*, 5–6).

Two later memories are connected with a boy nicknamed the Rat, whose gang made the storm sewers beneath the streets their particular playground. Once Eiseley and his friend were crawling their candle-lit way through the drains when, upon hearing the sound of rushing water above—and having no way of knowing until later that it was caused only by a fire hydrant being tested—they had the nightmarish experience of fearing that they would be trapped and drowned (*NC*, 21–24). On a subsequent occasion they found a moss-covered brick drain, large enough to stand upright in, that ran off into the darkness under a hill. This place they intended to keep just for the two of them, apart from the gang, but a few weeks after its discovery the other boy died of some unnamed childhood disease. One day after his friend's death Eiseley returned by himself to their secret entrance, the green door in the hillside. "But it was no use without the Rat," he writes. "I backed out and turned away" (*NC*, 25–26).

In still another episode the young Eiseley sought adventure under a bright autumn sky. Unseen by others, he climbed upon the back step of a horse-drawn tea wagon and went for a sunlit ride in the country. By the time the driver reached his destination, however, a storm had come up, and the journey that began with such promise ended with a rumble of thunder, the hollow rolling of wagon wheels on the stones of a drive, and the crash of closing iron gates. These sounds combined to echo through Eiseley's frightened head "with a kind of dreadful finality," and he was left to wait out the storm in a hedge beyond the grounds of a large house. Then, when the rain stopped, he was obliged to make the long walk homeward alone (*NC*, 7–10).

These episodes, filled with harshness, threat, and disappointment, turn out to be boyhood harbingers of Eiseley's experiences as a young man. His treatment of the latter extends over the eight-year period that began with his admission to the university in Lincoln, and ended with his departure from Nebraska in 1933, when he was beginning his twenty-seventh year and had finally earned his undergraduate degree.

In *All the Strange Hours* he presents three negative experiences as dominating the period. The first is the death of his father. Clyde had been dismissed from his job as a traveling hardware salesman, and when he returned home he already looked ill. Soon a strange lump appeared growing from his side, and the progress of the cancer eventually led to the welling up of a "black exudate of blood" at his lips (*ASH*, 17). It was devastating for Loren to watch his father die with agonizing slowness. When the end finally came, Eiseley discovered that he could no longer bear the ticking of the clock in his bedroom. "I used to lie for hours," he writes, "staring into the dark of the sleeping house, feeling the loneliness that only the sleepless know when the queer feeling comes that it is the sleeping who are alive and those awake are disembodied ghosts" (*NC*, 170). In this way he describes the onset of the insomnia that was to plague him for the rest of his life, a condition that he here associates with the trauma of his father's death.

Shortly after this event, we are told, Eiseley found employment in a chicken hatchery, where one of his jobs was the heaving of 150-pound sacks into the storeroom. At first this posed no problem, but before long he began to stagger under the weight of the sacks and to feel increasingly incapable of doing the work. When he later noticed that the color of his skin had turned gray, he went to the university dispensary (*ASH*, 19–20). There, according to his dramatic narrative, he was diagnosed as having tuberculosis, which meant that he now had to confront the possibility of his own early death. To combat the disease he first spent some time with an aunt in a rented cabin near Pike's Peak, where he could do nothing but wait in claustrophobic terror while his mind "raced endlessly upon itself" (*ASH*, 23). Then he was sent to the Mohave Desert. Although he had some contact with other people there, he says that he spent most of his time alone, living by himself in a cabin inhabited by pack rats who squealed overhead in a small attic during the long nights (*ASH*, 39).

A year of breathing the dry desert air healed his lungs, but the prolonged immobility and wary care of himself left him "savage, restless, at odds with his environment" (*ASH*, 47). Thus, when he returned to Lincoln, he was unable to force himself to complete the work necessary for graduation. Instead he took to riding the rails back and forth across the West along with many other of America's poor. Eiseley's narrative of this period in his life is memorable for the way it captures the violence and despair of the times in general. Although he recalls occasional acts of kindness, they are subordinate to the ever-present hunger, physical danger, and fierceness of others. The dominant lesson he learned from the experience, spelled out by one of the hoboes he met, is that "men beat men" (*ASH*, 12).

Combined with the difficulties of his childhood, these distressing experiences of his youth reflect a dark inner world of dislocation and increasing estrangement. Then, suddenly, that world was illuminated by the bright light of the high plains in western Nebraska. This happened as a result of Eiseley's becoming a member of the Morrill Paleontological Expeditions, a decision that—without his realizing it at the time—would at last enable him to stop spiraling downward. The fieldwork in which he took part, extending over the summers of 1931 through 1933, fired his imagination and allowed him to find a focus for his energies. According to his own testimony in the essays, it was the great watershed experience of his life. Wanting to climb over sand and stone in a desolate land, wanting to dig for the bones of creatures long dead, wanting to lie down beneath the inscrutable sky to consider the significance of life across the ages of geological time—all these are positive desires. Amid the sterile terrain of the Badlands, that place of death, Eiseley paradoxically came to life, or at least awoke to the possibility of a purposeful life for himself.

The material reviewed in the preceding pages, while not exhaustive, conveys (I believe) an accurate impression of Eiseley's presentation of himself as a child and young man. The account leaves him on the verge of a future he could not previously have anticipated, but before considering that we need to delve more deeply into the treatment of his past. For it is through the way he handles the people, places, and events of his early life that his personal myth emerges.

First of all it needs to be emphasized that Eiseley has no interest in providing an unadorned chronicle of his first twenty-six years. Instead, drawing upon the collection of pictures in the artist's loft of his mind, he verbalizes certain emotionally charged images, which he presents either in the form of brief descriptions or of more extended episodes. His method is impressionistic, one that usually avoids the sort of pedestrian details provided by public records in favor of references that serve to locate him within a grander framework.

Thus, in dedicating *The Night Country* to his grandmother Corey, he mentions that she "sleeps as all my people sleep by the ways of the westward crossing." And later in the book he says he was "conceived in and part of the rolling yellow cloud that . . . has been blowing in my part of the Middle West since the ice age" (*NC*, 197). Consider how different are the effects produced by these statements from those that would be conveyed by conventional notations of place and date of death (for his grandmother) and of birth (for himself). The first suggests that Eiseley was descended from a line of ancestors who were caught up in the sweep of a great historical movement, and the second places him within a geological context that transcends history. Neither statement is untrue, yet together they contribute to the weaving of a backdrop against which the emerging Eiseley figure looms larger than he would if the basic facts were to be presented in a more customary fashion.

Two childhood episodes, both conveying a destinal sense, will serve to illustrate the point in more detail. The first concerns a ruined farmhouse that Eiseley discovered one day after school. As he tells it,

> The road was one I had never taken before. Rain was falling. Leaves lay thick on the abandoned road. Hesitantly I approached and stood in the doorway. Plaster had collapsed from the ceiling; wind mourned through the empty windows. I crunched tentatively over shattered glass upon the floor. Papers lay scattered about in wild disorder. Some looked like school examination papers. I picked one up in curiosity, but this, my own mature judgment tells me, no one will believe. The name Eiseley was scrawled across the cover (*ASH*, 30).

It is difficult to accept this event at face value. Eiseley, it is true, anticipates our disbelief through the mention of his mature judgment. Yet there remains something excessively literary about the little narrative, as if it were filtered through the author's recollection of his reading in nineteenth-century gothic fiction. Furthermore there seems to be some factual confusion. One might well wonder how it is possible, if it was indeed raining, that in the very next paragraph Eiseley could see "the growing sunset through the window." On the other hand, we might explain away inconsistencies by conjecturing that the episode had its origin in a dream, one so vivid that it seemed to have taken place in the external world.

Yet, finally, we cannot settle these matters. All we have to go on are Eiseley's words. They may frustrate certain expectations about literalness of presentation in autobiography as opposed to fiction, but they nevertheless tell us something significant about Eiseley's way of viewing himself. The passage unmistakably conveys an intimation of dark, mysterious forces, forces that influence his life as an individual. It was an unknown road, let us recall, that led him to the abandoned building in the first place. And once there, after the shock of discovering the name of another Eiseley on a paper dated from "the last decade of the century before," he played alone with a pair of dice that he found in a corner. Unseen powers are again evoked. He asks, "For what stakes did I play, with my childish mind gravely considering?" Acknowledging that memory almost fails him, he answers, "I think I played against the universe as the universe was represented by the wind, stirring papers on the plaster-strewn floor. I played against time, . . . I played for adventure and escape" (*ASH*, 31).

Clearly the young boy could not have articulated such thoughts as these. They are instead those of the adult writer, who in part saw himself as a gambler in the game of life, but who also felt himself at a deeper level to have been singled out in his early years for some special (albeit uncertain) role in an enigmatic cosmic drama. Thus we come to understand that Eiseley uses the external narrative principally as a means of getting at an inner truth, as a way of dramatizing his essential, mythic self. And from this point of view the verifiability and consistency of the "facts" of the episode are irrelevant.

The second episode dates from 1910, the year of Halley's comet, and constitutes Eiseley's earliest recorded memory. "Like hundreds of other little boys of the new century," he writes, "I was held up in my father's arms under the cottonwoods of a cold and leafless spring to see the hurtling emissary of the void." Then he reports his father's words:

> "If you live to be an old man," he said carefully, fixing my eyes on the midnight spectacle, "you will see it again. It will come back in seventy-five years. Remember," he whispered in my ear, "I will be gone, but you will see it. All that time it will be traveling in the dark, but somewhere, far out there"—he swept a hand toward the blue horizon of the plains—"it will turn back. It is running glittering through millions of miles" (*IP*, 7).

Clinging tightly to his father's neck and staring without comprehension at the heavens, he heard his father say again, "I think you will live to see it—for me." Eiseley's own reply—"Yes, Papa"—amounted to a "desperate promise." It was given "out of love for a sad man who clung to me as I to him," he says, but in ignorance of what the future might hold in store (*IP*, 8).

As it turned out, Eiseley did not live to see the comet's return. While his inability to keep his promise was beyond his control, a reader might wish that he had better control over his facts. There can be no doubt that Halley's wandering star did visit our planet in 1910, but if Eiseley actually saw it in the spring of that year he would been have only two, not four years old, as he says. In any case he was very young, and could not possibly have recalled a long speech of his father's. From the perspective I have been developing here, however, the undiscoverable facts of the episode are not important. It is only the symbolic significance of the event that merits our attention.

To begin with the scene serves to strengthen our sense of the bond between father and son. This moment of closeness, we are led to believe, left an indelible impression on Eiseley, one that remained with him for the rest of his life. More importantly the episode lifts that life out of the ordinary, for here Eiseley portrays himself from the very beginning as an actor on a cosmic stage. "Because of my father and the promise I had made," he writes, "a kind of personal bond [was] projected between me and the comet." Did he not become a ponderer of the void, and still more memorably a poet-scientist of time? No wonder, he implies; there were signs. The star dragon (as he calls the comet) had marked him, fixing him with "the compulsive vertigo of vast distance and even more endless time," and thereby determining in a sense the course of his future (*IP*, 8–9).

Turning now from an examination of particular episodes to a consideration of Eiseley's past as a whole, we find ourselves inevitably struck by another aspect of his purported memories—their almost unrelieved grimness. The only light to be seen in his dark past is the aureole surrounding his idealized father. Otherwise most of the images are harsh and forbidding, images whose cumulative effect is overwhelmingly negative. The implication is that beyond the control of the boy and young man there were powerful forces at work that tended toward his destruction. According to the story Eiseley tells, his escape into a stable, productive life in adulthood was a narrow one.

Yet the stark memorability of this story is made possible because of the autobiographer's insistence on exclusion, on the chiseling away of pieces of his life that do not suit his purpose. What are told, for example, about the years between his prepubertal days as an explorer of the storm drains and his entrance into the University of Nebraska? Almost nothing. Through a reading of Gale Christianson's work, however, we learn that Mamie, the wife of Loren's older half-brother Leo, for a while assuaged the growing boy's loneliness. During the two years that she lived in Lincoln (1920–22), she became his confidante and encouraged him to talk openly about his problems. Furthermore Eiseley seems to have blossomed socially in high school, especially in his senior year, when he was captain of the football team and president of his class. He was friendly then with a dozen or so classmates, both girls and boys, who passed time in a favorite cafe in downtown Lincoln and attended parties on weekends. With three of these boys he also spent a memorable postgraduation summer (1925) riding around the West in an unreliable Model-T Ford they named "Old Purgatory."

Eiseley himself likewise says nothing to temper his somber account of the eight-year period beginning with his admission to the university. Once again we have to look elsewhere to learn of his warm association with Lowery Wimberly, the founding editor of the *Prairie Schooner*, and with the group of students (including Wilbur Gaffney) who were drawn into the Wimberly circle. And only in the recent biography of Eiseley do we get an extended account of daily life on the fossil-hunting expeditions in western Nebraska. While it is true that the region itself was lonely, a great deal of camaraderie developed among those who went there. Yet Eiseley honors these friendships only once, in the dedication to *The Innocent Assassins*, his first collection of poems, which reads: "To the bone hunters of the old South Party, Morrill Expeditions 1931–1933, and to C. Bertrand Schultz, my comrade of those years, this book in memory of the unreturning days."

Other people who were important to him during his erratic undergraduate days are also ignored. He says nothing about his various love interests, for instance, or about his friendship with several women belonging to the family of one of his good friends at the time. In addition he has little to say about members of his own family who helped him during his difficult youth. He might dedicate his autobiography to William Buchanan Price, the uncle "without whose help my life would have been different beyond imagining," but that man figures hardly at all in the book itself. And the same is true of Price's wife, Daisy's sister, who stayed with the young man in Colorado after his lung condition was diagnosed. The fact that such people as these are not felt presences in any of Eiseley's books in part accounts for why the destructive forces mentioned above appear so monolithic and menacing.

All autobiographies, as we have seen, have to be selective, but this raises a question about the principle of selection that underlies the writing. A partial answer in Eiseley's case is provided by his own account, previously referred to, of a writer's mind. Because certain pictures or images insist upon themselves in a way that is beyond the individual's control, all the writer can do is undertake the task of trying to draw meaning out of them in his work.

In the course of this undertaking, however, the autobiographer inevitably develops a view of himself and his life. It comes about because of the configurations which form as he ruminates upon the images that constitute his raw material. Once this happens, once an identifiable gestalt emerges, he then has a conscious basis for making decisions about what to include in his writing. And he may well feel, given the dictates of his artistic sense, that anything which does not fit the patterns of meaning he has discovered should be left out.

It seems likely that Loren Eiseley underwent a process of this sort. In any case, a close reading of his essays reveals that by the time he reached his maturity as a writer he had established a dominant view of himself as a castaway, a fugitive, and a solitary wanderer. With his talent for thinking metaphorically, Eiseley draws connections between the external meanings literally denoted by the three words *castaway-fugitive-wanderer* and his own inner condition, which is chiefly characterized by a profound sense of homelessness.

The source of the first of these identity labels can be traced back to *Robinson Crusoe*. When Eiseley was five Leo came home for a brief visit, and while there began reading the novel aloud. "I lived for that story," Eiseley tells us. "I hung upon my brother's words." But Leo left before finishing the work and Loren "proceeded to worry and chew [his] way like a puppy through the remaining pages" (*ASH*, 173). This was the first book he ever read, and it made a lifelong impression upon him. For in Defoe's shipwrecked hero he later came to find a powerful image of the human condition. As he wrote in his own first book, "On the world island we are all castaways" (*IJ*, 14).

The force of the castaway image for Eiseley is undoubtedly also connected with his childhood situation in general. In a sense, as his early memories suggest, it was difficult for him to feel "at home." To reinforce the idea he calls himself a changeling, because he was the belated offspring of his father's unfortunate middle-aged marriage. Leo, on the other hand—the child of Clyde's youth, of his marriage to a beloved woman who died young—was in Eiseley's mind "the one true son" (*ASH*, 15). Feelings of this sort are likely to leave an enduring mark upon the character and can surface in unexpected ways in later life. In referring to the evolutionary habit of thought he acquired in adulthood, for instance, Eiseley mentions being overcome on one occasion with a monstrous vision of the mythical tree of Igdrasil, which he describes in these words: "It writhes, it crawls, it barks and snuffles and roars . . . [while] shaping itself endlessly out of darkness toward the light" (*FT*, 168). This way of seeing, he then explains, opened such a strange world in his brain that it made him "a castaway," one who had "no refuge in time, as others do who troop homeward at nightfall" (*FT*, 169).

Linked to the castaway is the fugitive who, instead of being deprived of home by some outside force, flees of his own accord. At the start of *The Night Country* Eiseley anticipates criticism from those who would say that "fugitives are made by laws and acts of violence, that without these preliminaries no man can be called a fugitive." Rejecting this legalistic view, he asserts that some men come into the world to hunt and some to flee, "whether physically or mentally makes no difference." And in no uncertain terms he declares where he stands: "I am a fugitive. I was born one" (*NC*, 4). Early evidence of this impulse is reflected in his account of the tea-wagon journey and of the episode in which he ran away from his mother. Later he picks up the motif again by identifying himself, in retrospect, with Tom Murry, an escaped convict who was pursued and killed in the darkness of a Nebraska winter (*ASH*, 28). Like Murry, Eiseley sees himself within his mind as a running man, far from lamplight and warmth, vainly trying to flee from a universe in which he too would finally be hunted down.

Lastly there is the wanderer, who adds one more dimension to our trio of identity figures. Like the other two he is also solitary and homeless, but his chief desire is to recover what he has lost. Once again Eiseley enhances his motif through mythological allusion, referring to Odysseus as the archetype of "homeward-yearning man," the seeker after a "spiritual home" that is ever denied him (*UU*, 4). Sympathetically he quotes the desperate outcry of Homer's hero—"There is nothing worse for men than wandering" (*UU*, 5)—but he sees it as inherent in the human condition. We cannot *not* seek, he suggests. Certainly he could not, and his books contain the record of his unceasing personal quest.

How are we to understand the desire for a recovery of loss in Eiseley? On the one hand, given the childhood memories presented earlier, it may seem that—apart from the love of his father—he had little enough to lose. Yet he is not wholly consistent in his account of those years. He has a treasured recollection, for instance, of "a rare moment of doting agreement" between his parents. It occurred when they decided not to send him to kindergarten in order that he could be free to play for one more year. He recalls a soft inflection in their voices and remembers that the two of them "smiled in sudden affection" (*ASH*, 172). More extraordinarily, in a late poem called "The Mist on the Mountain," he expresses an aching desire not only to return to his childhood home but also to be as he was then. He pictures himself at age five with his parents, reading at the lamplit, oilcloth-covered table in the kitchen, and laments the passage of time. "Father, mother, take me back," he cries. While acknowledging the harshness of life in those days, he feels it to have been far preferable to his later years spent in an "alien, grown-up body." And the poem ends with a fantasy of wish fulfillment: "I have rushed like a moth through time / toward the light in the kitchen. / I am safe now. I never grew up" (*IA*, 113–15).

As this poem suggests, the loss Eiseley has in mind is an inner one, one that is inherent in the process of growing up. Elsewhere he mentions the innocence of the very young, saying, "I am always amazed at this aspect of creation, the small Eden that does not last, but recurs with the young of every generation" (*ASH*, 159). The biblical allusion here reminds us that the loss is embodied in one of the seminal myths of Western civilization. Although the paradisal garden was for centuries believed by many to have a physical location somewhere in the external world, just as the ancient Greeks and Romans envisioned the Golden Age as having existed at some time long gone, we now find it meaningful to interpret the story psychologically. As Joseph Campbell has written, "Taken as referring not to any geographical scene, but to a landscape of the soul [the] Garden of Eden would have to be within us. Yet our conscious minds are unable to enter it and enjoy there the taste of eternal life, since we have already tasted of the knowledge of good and evil. That, in fact, must then be the knowledge that has thrown us out of the garden, pitched us away from our own center."

In the light of this understanding we can see that two of Eiseley's childhood memories have symbolic significance, being presented as parables of the Fall. The first is the turtle-killing episode that occurred, we are told, in Green Gulch. This sandstone basin was secluded and quiet, "with trees leaning secretly inward" above a pool, and with "green ferns touching the green water." The boys played "innocently" there, until they found the huge turtle, "the spirit of the place," who was "the last lord of the green water before the town poured over it." Then came the horrific killing of that spirit by creatures who, seeming no longer human, next turned their vicious, gnomelike faces upon Eiseley and drove him away from the green world. This experience, he says, brought about his discovery of evil, which was "a monstrous and corroding knowledge" (*NC*, 5–6).

The other pertinent memory is of the ride on the tea wagon. At the beginning of this episode Eiseley emphasizes the color gold in the same way that he stresses green in the previous one. The wagon wheels themselves were golden, he says, and "[w]hen the horse broke into a spanking trot those wheels spun and glittered in the equally golden air of autumn with an irresistible attraction." It was thus a "marvelous ride" that he took into the open countryside through "the kind of eternal light which exists only in the minds of the very young" (*NC*, 8–9).

As we have previously seen, however, the journey ended with a disturbing cacaphony of sounds. In addition Eiseley remained outside the iron fence enclosing the grounds of the bishop's house—the driver's destination—which to his childish mind seemed to contain a "somewhat supernatural world." Seeking protection from the storm within a hedge beside the entrance, he became aware that he was not alone, that hundreds of brown birds were hidden there, "immersed in a kind of waiting silence so secret and immense that I was much too overawed to disturb them." When the storm was over, all he could do (as in the aftermath of the earlier episode) was to walk back to town alone, feeling in the process "some obscure sense of loss" (*NC*, 9–10).

Fundamental to the Garden-of-Eden story is the idea of paradise lost, and both of Eiseley's parables contain this universal theme. In the Green Gulch episode he is driven away from an idyllic locale into which the knowledge of evil had entered, and in the tea-wagon tale he endures three distinct exclusions: from the eternal light of the marvelous ride, from the supernatural domain of the bishop's house, and from the mysterious world of the birds (who are themselves at one with their surroundings). In both cases innocence gives way to experience, but his mind harbors a lingering awareness of the former, which manifests itself in adulthood as a hunger for innocence, for the recovery of Eden, for a spiritual home. "The origins of this hunger," Eiseley admits, "are as mysterious as the reasons why we, who are last year's dust and rain, have risen from that dust to look about with the devised crystal of a raindrop before we subside once more into snow and whirling vapor" (*ASH*, 146). Yet there can be no doubt that this hunger gnawed at him; it is what made him the wanderer or pilgrim he became.

Our understanding of these and other episodes from Eiseley's past is enhanced if we bring to bear upon them a key distinction that Edwin Muir makes in his own autobiography, the distinction between story and fable. The former is what we most commonly assume constitutes an autobiography—that is, the story of a life, an account of its beginnings and of its development through time up to the point of the writing. Muir acknowledges that this is a necessary part of the autobiographer's task, and he devotes most of his book to it. Yet he knows there is more to life than the facts or phenomena of his ordinary existence. Of that part of himself he says, "I know [it] in an external and deceptive way, as if it were a dry legend which I had made up in collusion with mankind." The other dimension of life, the deeper, less time-bound one, is harder to get at, but it is connected with Muir's conviction that "the life of every man is an endlessly repeated performance of the life of man." He elaborates in this fashion:

> In themselves our conscious lives may not be particularly interesting. But what we are not and can never be, our fable, seems to be inconceivably interesting. I should like to write that fable, but I cannot even live it; and all I could do if I related the outward course of my life would be to show how I have deviated from it; though even that is impossible, since I do not know the fable or anybody who knows it. One or two stages in it I can recognize: the age of innocence and the Fall and all the dramatic consequences which issue from the Fall. But these lie behind experience, not on its surface; they are not historical events; they are stages in the fable.

To my knowledge Loren Eiseley had not read these words, but he clearly shares Muir's viewpoint. And from that point of view we can see that he does more than select and arrange his memories for the sake of artistic effect. He also often presents them in such a way as to provide suggestions of the fable or myth that lies behind the individual circumstances of his past. For Eiseley, too, the "dry legend" is not enough. He believes a deeper vision is needed in order to convey a true sense of his life, an impression of the way his life was in its essence.

We might say, then, that the surface details of Eiseley's life as he depicts them are fraught with intimations of depth. Muir does his best to explain this elusive notion here, and more will be said about it in Chapter 4. Here, however, it is enough to say that this depth dimension—to the extent that Eiseley is successful in evoking it—contributes to the portrayal of a protagonist who goes beyond the ordinary, whose stature seems large than life-size.

Another method Eiseley uses to accomplish this end is the association of himself with figures of mythic proportions. Two of these, Odysseus and Robinson Crusoe, have already been mentioned. Yet there is a third figure—Ishmael—who is even more emblematic of his life. Ishmael's origins, of course, are biblical: the son of Abraham by the handmaid Hagar, he is cast out from his people and thereafter dwells in the wilderness. This last detail is significant because, as the next chapter will show, Eiseley makes much of the wilderness theme in regard to his own life. But Ishmael has even greater connection to Eiseley because of Melville's adaptation of the ancient character. In *Moby-Dick* Ishmael is not only a wanderer across a watery wilderness, but also a contemplative man and a tale teller.

Portrayed as a shipboard philosopher, Ishmael often meditates upon the nature of human existence, and there is one passage in particular that merits special notice here. At the end of the chapter called "Brit" he addresses the reader directly, saying,

> [C]onsider them both, the sea and the land; and do you not find a strange analogy to something in yourself? For as this appalling ocean surrounds the verdant land, so in the soul of man there lies one insular Tahiti, full of peace and joy, but encompassed by all the horrors of the half known life. God keep thee! Push not off from that isle, thou canst never return!

In the light of material presented above, it is easy to picture Eiseley agreeing with these words, sadly recognizing their applicability to his own life. Moreover, in "Science and the Sense of the Holy," which contains some discussion of *Moby-Dick*, Eiseley explicitly identifies himself with Melville's narrator. Both are wanderers, he observes, and both tell stories about what they have seen and thought and felt as a result of their travels, whether made in body or in mind. Quoting Melville quoting the Book of Job, he ends the essay with the words, "I only am escaped to tell thee" (*ST*, 201).

If we now reconsider Eiseley's storied past, it is evident that the early experiences he recounts all make their contribution to the development of a modern Ishmael. Given the images of childhood and youth I have shown you, he seems to say, is it any wonder I became the isolate I did? Yet, just as Melville's character escaped the deadly whirlpool created by the sinking of the doomed *Pequod*, so Eiseley managed to avoid being caught up in the vortex of those events and circumstances that threatened to destroy him. This escape was made possible chiefly by his sojourn in remote landscapes.

Prior to going on his first paleontological expedition, we remember, Eiseley presents himself as having reached the nadir of affliction. Three years before he had suffered the death of his father, which separated him from the only person he claims to have loved at the time. Next, because of the tubercular threat to his own life, he had endured separation from health and the normal vigor of youth. In desperation he then began riding the rails in the West, an activity indicative of his separation from a settled social order and a sense of purpose in life. Atop the freight cars and amid the hobo camps he became a castaway among thousands of social outcasts, a fugitive with no particular place to hide. Such utterly aimless movement makes manifest Eiseley's homelessness, which by that time had become a spiritual as well as a physical condition.

This is the low point in the story that he tells about his past, the point of futility and despair. Yet even futility and despair have their uses. As Henry James, Sr., once observed in writing to his sons, "The natural inheritance of everyone who is capable of spiritual life is an unsubdued forest where the wolf howls and the obscene bird of night chatters." Although that forest and its threatening inhabitants haunted Eiseley all his life, a fortuitous event—as often happens in accounts of spiritual journeys—was soon to pull him up out of the depths to which he had fallen at this time. The event came in the form of an invitation to join a party of fossil hunters, which, in retrospect, may well have seemed like an act of destiny to Eiseley. For by accepting it the future "student of desolation" (*UU*, 214) was led to find a physical correlative of his inner world, an external landscape ideally suited to his psyche.

It is probably safe to assume that the young man who actually did fieldwork in western Nebraska experienced feelings he could not articulate at the time. Yet the work itself so captured his interest that he was prompted to attend graduate school in anthropology and then move on to a university career. That he should become a professional student of the earth's obscure history would have been an inconceivable possibility to the youth who a few years before had ridden the rails with America's destitute. The distance from the Badlands to Philadelphia could not for Eiseley be measured in miles alone. Nevertheless, proving himself to be both a successful teacher and productive scholar, academic life suited him well.

More importantly, given the literary work for which he has become most famous, it provided him with the opportunity he needed to read and to think. Only after long study and reflection was the mature writer able to suggest linkages between his own condition and past, and the condition and past of the planet. He had felt thwarted within himself, for example; there (in western Nebraska) he saw a sandchoked landscape with his outward-looking eyes. He had experienced a wasteland of the spirit; there he beheld a barren land in the external world. He had traveled a dark road from the time of his earliest childhood recollections to the present; there he surveyed a terrain whose visible surface covered the murky evidence of an incredibly distant past.

All this may seem like cold comfort, but the value to Eiseley of the discovery of such analogical connections between the microcosm of himself and the macrocosm of the earth can scarcely be overestimated. Paleontological fieldwork, combined with broad scientific learning and poetic insight, enabled him to find the larger context of signification for which his spirit yearned. Without it he presumably would have been overwhelmed by the forces of meaninglessness. With it he established himself as the brooding hero of his personal myth. And it is this figure—the wanderer or solitary seeker who, with Sisyphean perseverence, refuses to give up his struggle despite the threat of ultimate extinction—that captures our imaginations.

III

Readings in the Book of Nature

> Say what some poets will, Nature is not so much her own ever-sweet interpreter, as the mere supplier of that cunning alphabet, whereby selecting and combining as he pleases, each man reads his own peculiar lesson according to his own peculiar mind and mood.
>
> —Herman Melville

In a discarded introduction to *The Night Country* Eiseley declares, "I lived these hours whether of action or of thought." The story of his childhood and youth, as we have seen, contains a good deal of the former. It begins with his origins in a dark house, moves through the years in which various external experiences make their formative marks upon him, and culminates in the Badlands where the young man's eyes are opened to new possibilities. Since from the vantage point of the present the future is always opaque, the path that lay before him was of course obscure at that time. Looking back, however, with all of his books open to us, we can see that the hours Eiseley was to live as an adult were most significantly ones of thought. His mature essays record the movements of a nomad of the mind.

Many would argue that such writing can scarcely be considered autobiographical. It is this outlook that has prompted some translators to publish editions of Augustine's *Confessions* containing only its first nine books, wherein the saint recounts the story of his past up to the time of his conversion. Yet not all autobiographical writing need be retrospective. In Book X of the *Confessions* Augustine directly scrutinizes his inner condition at the time of the writing, and his meditations on the opening of Genesis in the last three books also reveal a great deal about his temperament and habits of mind. Montaigne provides another outstanding case in point, for he came to see that in his collected essays he had produced a book "consubstantial with its author." In his mind the two were one, and we who live four centuries after his death can best come to know the man by reading his book.

The same is true of Loren Eiseley. While we can trace the main outlines of his career in *All the Strange Hours*, it is the evocation of the essential life of the author that is most memorable and significant in his works. And this is as it should be because, as Georges Gusdorf has written, "in autobiography the truth of facts is subordinate to the truth of the man, for it is first of all the man who is in question." Writing of this sort cannot be neatly plotted, but it nevertheless tells a special kind of inner story. Consequently, as we explore the world of Eiseley's essays, we inevitably come to a deepened understanding of the man who through the written word mentally explored the world around him.

In *The Human Venture* Gerald Heard lists three cardinal questions that human beings have sought to answer: "(1) *Where am I*? What is the character of my natural setting? (2) *What am I*? How am I related to other men? (3) *Who am I*? What is the nature and final destiny of this consciousness which is the core of my being?" He goes on to explain that these questions—which call attention, respectively, to nature, society, and the self—have not been given equal consideration historically by the world's three major cultures. China focused on the second one, the question of association; India emphasized the third, the question of integration; and the West, which was the last to emerge, stressed the first, the question of orientation.

If we narrow the application of Heard's categories to Loren Eiseley as an individual man, we find that he shows some interest in society at large. This is especially true of *The Invisible Pyramid*, in which he utters dire warnings about the dangers posed to human welfare by institutionalized science. In addition we learn of his social conservatism because of the negative comments he makes in various places about the sixties generation in America. But the more fundamental matter of the individual's association with other human beings is avoided almost entirely once he passes beyond his youth. Thus the concern signaled by Heard's second question is conspicuous because of the way Eiseley excludes it from consideration in his essays.

Since other people play so small a role in his work, we might expect to find an intense concentration on Heard's third question. Yet this is not so. Although Eiseley's voice dominates every page he wrote, it is not turned inwardly upon himself. The Indian concern with consciousness, even in the modern form of psychological self-analysis, is alien to him. Despite the fact that *All the Strange Hours* is subtitled "The Excavation of a Life," we read in vain if we expect to find overt explorations of his own psyche.

What we find instead is a preoccupation with the first question: *Where* am I? Place, of course, is vital to all children, no matter where or when they are born. Who we were in our earliest years is so intimately bound up with where we were, that the two are virtually coextensive. It is therefore impossible to imagine the young Eiseley apart from the home life and street life in Nebraska that he describes. By presenting his early environment so concretely Eiseley demonstrates the life-writer's need to ground himself. In this respect, as Janet Varner Gunn has pointed out, autobiography embodies the story of the mythical Antaeus, whose invincibility was assured as long as he kept in contact with the earth. Thus understood, autobiographical writing is "an act of orientation" in which "[t]he question of the self's identity becomes a question of the self's location in the world."

Our interest in that question obviously persists beyond childhood. In Western culture, especially, it manifests itself in an overriding concern with our common dwelling place, the natural world.

And, as Heard points out, this concern has led to "that experimentation with nature that has culminated in modern science."

Despite his professional training and the success of his career, however, Eiseley was never wholly comfortable with modern science, at least not as typified by its most disciplined laboratory devotees. In "The Enchanted Glass," an essay-review published in the same year as his first book (1957), he isolates two attitudes toward nature that have been evident in Western culture since the seventeenth century. The first, for which Francis Bacon is the principal early spokesman, he calls "severely experimental, unaesthetic, and empirical." The other, which he associates with Thoreau and other chiefly nineteenth-century figures, "is literary, personal, and contemplative" (*EG*, 478). Two decades later, in "Science and the Sense of the Holy," Eiseley reaffirmed the same dichotomy by writing:

> In the end science as we know it has two basic types of practitioners. One is the educated man who still has a controlled sense of wonder before the universal mystery, whether it hides in a snail's eye or within the light that impinges on that delicate organ. The second kind of observer is the extreme reductionist who is so busy stripping things apart that the tremendous mystery has been reduced to a trifle, to intangibles not worth troubling one's head about (*ST*, 190).

These passages make it clear where Eiseley himself stands. His complaint against the strict Baconian type of scientist is that he is "apt to find himself more and more removed from visible nature and its emotional connotations, more and more preoccupied with the inner constituents of things, until he has literally dissolved them away into fields of force, warps in space, or other abstractions" (*EG*, 480). By temperament Eiseley takes a much less detached approach to nature, one that puts him in agreement with Alfred North Whitehead, who once wrote:

> When you understand all about the sun and all about the atmosphere and all about the rotation of the earth, you may still miss the radiance of the sunset. There is no substitute for the direct perception of the concrete achievement of a thing in its actuality. We want concrete fact with a high light thrown upon what is relevant to its preciousness.

Eiseley therefore favors "the old-fashioned contemplative naturalist," who tells "an essentially personal story" in which are recorded "the shifting colors in the enchanted glass of the mind." These experiences, as he further points out, have more than an individual value because they are "capable of being shared by every perceptive human being. They are part of that indefinable country which lies between the realm of natural objects and the human spirit which moves among them" (*EG*, 480).

As the publication of *The Immense Journey* made clear, Eiseley himself was the very sort of contemplative naturalist he describes here. His declared purpose in that book was to provide "the record of what one man thought as he pursued research and pressed his hands against the confining walls of scientific method in his time" (*IJ*, 13). Instead of aiming primarily for a readership of fellow academics, he wanted to share with a wider audience "the prowlings of one mind which has sought to explore, to understand, and to enjoy the miracles of this world, both in and out of science" (*IJ*, 12). Miracles? It is not a word that many scientists would use, and such talk undoubtedly contributed to making him "a stranger in [his] own department," as he acknowledged in a different context (*ASH*, 132). A comment of this sort enables us to understand the professional price he had to pay for listening to his inner voice, but the rest of us—readers eager to gain a foothold in the "indefinable country" of which he wrote—are the beneficiaries of his willingness to pay whatever it cost.

Eiseley is one of a goodly number of modern writers who share his concerns. Aldo Leopold (in *Sand County Almanac*), for example, along with Edward Abbey (in *Desert Solitaire*), Gary Snyder (in *Turtle Island*), and Annie Dillard (in *Pilgrim at Tinker Creek*) all belong to that flourishing genre of American literature that John C. Elder has labeled "naturalist autobiography." Yet Eiseley pays no attention to these contemporaries in his own work. This may be because he felt his deepest kinship, as Andrew Angyal has suggested, with certain "gifted Victorians," men of science who could also write with eloquence about the natural world. At any rate, to get our bearings in the territory Eiseley made his own, we will be helped most by establishing some points of reference among the earlier literary naturalists to whom he first pays homage in "The Enchanted Glass."

In doing so, the first thing we notice is the importance of *place* in all their writings. Without exception they implicitly asked themselves Heard's first question: Where am I? And each of them answered it by looking closely at, and responding sensitively to, his immediate surroundings. For two native Englishmen, Gilbert White (1720–93) and Richard Jefferies (1848–87), the places were, respectively, Selborne in Hampshire and Coate in Wiltshire. W. H. Hudson (1841–1922), although he wrote memorably about locales in England as well, laid special claim to the pampas of Argentina, where he spent the first twenty-eight years of his life. More significant than these three, however, is America's own H. D. Thoreau (1817–62), the writer-naturalist about whom Eiseley has more to say than any other. *Walden* will therefore serve as our most revealing reference point in connection with Eiseley's own essays.

The special importance and value of place to certain individuals is explicitly recognized by Eiseley in two pieces on the poet Robinson Jeffers. "No one reading Jeffers," he comments in the later of the two, "can escape the impress of the untamed Pacific environment upon which he brooded. . . . The sea-beaten coast, the fierce freedom of its hunting hawks, possessed and spoke through him. It was one of the most uncanny and complete relationships between man and his natural background that I know in literature." The only literary naturalist he specifically names as being comparable to Jeffers in this regard is Thoreau. What we have in both cases, as Eiseley recognized while still an undergraduate, is "the complete identification of the individual with his environment, or, rather, the extension of the environment into the individual to such a degree that the latter seems almost a lens, a gathering point through which, in some psychic and unexplainable manner, is projected a portion of the diversified and terrific forces of nature that otherwise stream helplessly away without significance to humanity."

Individuals who can serve this lenslike function are few in number. Not only must they be gifted in the use of words in order to communicate with the rest of us; they must also (in Eiseley's view) feel the call of the wilderness. The idea of wilderness is so basic to the Eiseleyan outlook, and is so closely bound up with the Ishmael theme, that we need to clarify our understanding of it before going any further.

According to the *Oxford English Dictionary*, the word "wilderness" has two distinguishable literal meanings. First, in contrast to the desert, which is uninhabitable and uncultivatable, it can simply identify land that is still wild or uncultivated. This is the sense the word has when people speak of the need to protect wilderness areas from the encroachments of industrial civilization. Like W. H. Hudson before him, Eiseley, along with a host of contemporary writers, was sympathetic to this need. In *The Invisible Pyramid* he repeatedly refers to wilderness thus understood as "the green world" or "the sunflower forest" in order to distinguish it from the secondary world of human culture. "Today man's mounting numbers and his technological power to pollute his environment," he warns, "reveal a single demanding necessity: the necessity for him consciously to reenter and preserve, for his own safety, the old first world from which he originally emerged" (*IP*,154).

In its second literal sense "wilderness" denotes a waste or desolate region of any kind, including the open sea. Used in this way, however, the word comes laden with associations that have gathered around it over the course of centuries. As a result it easily crosses the indistinct borderline between the literal and the figurative, and it is in this sense that Eiseley's employment of the word has the most resonance.

At the beginning of "The Judgment of the Birds," for instance, he writes:

> It is a commonplace of all religious thought, even the most primitive, that the man seeking visions and insight must go apart from his fellows and live for a time in the wilderness. If he is of the proper sort, he will return with a message. It may not be a message from the god he set out to seek, but even if he has failed in that particular, he will have had a vision or seen a marvel, and these are always worth listening to and thinking about (*IJ*, 163).

Behind this paragraph lies our knowledge of an event such as the forty days that Jesus is said to have spent in the wilderness, during which period the devil appeared three times to tempt him. Or we may recall the traditional practice of various American Indian tribes, wherein youths preparing for manhood are sent on solitary vision quests in isolated areas.

Experiences of the sort just described are temporary; it is expected that the individuals will return to the communities they left. Yet not all wilderness sojourns can be so neatly planned, simply because it is not hard to lose one's way in unmapped territory. Consequently, as the dictionary entry points out, wilderness easily acquires a figurative sense referring to any place that one finds desolate, or in which one feels lonely or lost. Dante makes use of the concept in this way when, at the start of *The Divine Comedy*, he depicts himself as waking in a dark wood. On the literal story level of the poem the wood is really there, but it clearly also refers to a region of the spirit in which the pilgrim Dante unhappily finds himself in the middle of his life.

Near the beginning of *The Immense Journey* Eiseley also employs the word in a figurative sense when he says, "I can at best report only from my own wilderness" (*IJ*, 13). Since his declared intention is to record "such miracles as can be evoked from common earth," the term has positive, hopeful connotations in this context. Yet elsewhere his use of the word has much more somber implications. In his foreword to *The Night Country*, for example, he mentions that the contents of the book have been "drawn from many times and places in the wilderness of a single life," and that in arranging the essays his thoughts were "all of night, of outer cold and inner darkness" (*NC*, xi). Here he is in a Dantean mood, a man inhabiting a dark, desolate region from which he cannot escape.

Ishmael is an archetype of this figure, for the biblical character went to live in the wilderness only because he had no choice. He and his mother would never have left Abraham voluntarily, since in traditional cultures an individual's life loses its meaning apart from the clan. This is well illustrated in "The Wanderer," an Old English poem in which the sole survivor of a certain people, sailing alone in an open boat, laments his fate. Odysseus at least had the hope of getting home eventually, of returning to his wife, his son, and his countrymen. With that hope denied him, the Anglo-Saxon thane can only give haunting expression (in the Raffel translation) to his utter despair:

> I've drunk too many lonely dawns,
> Grey with mourning. Once there were men
> To whom my heart could hurry, hot
> With open longing. They're long since dead.
> My heart has closed on itself, quietly
> Learning that silence is noble and sorrow
> Nothing that speech can cure.

But by the mid-nineteenth century the changes wrought in Western sensibility by the romantic movement had brought about a reversal of the traditional situation. In literature as in life individuals felt impelled to separate themselves from communities that no longer seemed to nurture and support them. Thus Thoreau, in a dramatic gesture, went to live for two years and more in a woodland hut, hoping to dig beneath the mud and slush of opinion, prejudice, tradition, delusion, and appearance in order to find Reality. For him society had become the entity against which, rather than within which, he needed to define himself. Physically, at least, Melville's Ishmael went still further. He left the land altogether, that place where on weekdays thousands upon thousands of men are "pent up in lath and plaster—tied to counters, nailed to benches, clinched to desks." Daily living in society, in other words, had become trivial and stultifying—a kind of imprisonment. Desiring to revive his spirit, Ishmael therefore embarked upon a voyage across the watery wilderness, a voyage on which he explicitly sought "the ungraspable phantom of life."

Eiseley made forays into geographical wilderness areas chiefly during his youth in Nebraska. But for him the most significant wilderness was the realm where the individual soul encounters the world. And in that zone he could derive no comfort from the physical presence of others. On the contrary, although he made his home for three decades in a suburb of Philadelphia, he has no good things to say about life in such an environment. Psychologically he always remained an outsider, an isolated wanderer in a densely populated wasteland, one who sought "the ungraspable phantom of life" through the dark and incessant probings of his own restless mind.

Equipped with this understanding of wilderness and the Ishmael theme, we are now in a better position to consider Eiseley in the context of those literary naturalists to whom he specifically calls our attention. Three of them are no longer very familiar to American readers, and of that number the one most distantly connected to Eiseley is Gilbert White. His *Natural History of Selborne*, first published in 1789, is one of the classics in the tradition of British nature writing, and it is as impossible to think of him apart from his little village as it is Thoreau apart from Walden Pond. But White's treatment of his natural surroundings is preromantic. As an eighteenth-century man, he always remains the unsentimental observer.

Reading White's book, we discover that its author was primarily motivated by an unquenchable curiosity. Thus he can furnish lists of birds from his own observations in his neighborhood—of migratory birds, for instance, or birds that remain in full song after midsummer, or those that sing as they fly. He is also able to produce a five-page monograph on the house-martin, and do a similar job for the swallow. Yet, as he acknowledges in a letter of 1779, "It is now more than forty years that I have paid some attention to the ornithology of this district, without being able to exhaust the subject: new occurrences still arise as long as any inquiries are kept alive."

A reader of *The Natural History of Selborne* inevitably receives the stamp of its author's character, which is what Eiseley means by saying that the literary naturalist tells a personal story. In White's case the style of the book reveals a man whose inquisitiveness is never overbearing. On the contrary he is characterized by an endearing geniality, by a low-keyed readiness to be delighted as well as instructed by whatever he encounters.

Two illustrative passages will help to fix the man in our minds. The first concerns an old tortoise named Timothy who was observed while digging his hibernaculum. White notes: "It scrapes out the ground with it's fore-feet, and throws it up over it's back with it's hind; but the motion of it's legs is ridiculously slow, little exceeding the hour-hand of a clock; and suitable to the composure of an animal said to be a whole month in performing one feat of copulation." The second passage, a self-contained one-paragraph story, appears in the midst of some comments White makes on frogs and toads. He writes:

> I have been informed also, from undoubted authority, that some ladies (ladies you will say of peculiar taste) took a fancy to a toad, which they nourished summer after summer, for many years, till he grew to a monstrous size, with the maggots which turn to flesh flies. The reptile used to come forth every evening from an hole under the garden-steps; and was taken up, after supper, on the table to be fed. But at last a tame raven, kenning him as he put forth his head, gave him such a severe stroke with his horny beak as put out one eye. After this accident the creature languished for some time and died.

What could be more revealing? Here nature is so domesticated that the question "Where am I?" is free from any suggestion of terror. Gilbert White is no Ishmael, and the idea of wilderness is apparently alien to him. His attraction for us resides instead in his unselfconscious portrait of a man entirely at ease on his sequestered patch of earth, the place that for him was home.

The preceding chapter suggests how different this is from Eiseley's sense of homelessness. Another indication of the gap in sensibility between the two men is provided by the opening sentences of *The Firmament of Time*, a book whose title is taken from a poem by Shelley. There Eiseley writes, "Man is at heart a romantic. He believes in thunder, the destruction of worlds, the voice out of the whirlwind" (*FT*, 3). Yet not even all romantics need have the penchant for darkness and violence revealed here, and Richard Jefferies is a good case in point.

Born in the hamlet of Coate near Swindon, Jefferies spent the first twenty-nine years of his life in Wiltshire. His early journalistic writings, collected to form several books, show him to have been an excellent field naturalist in the manner of White, and a fine recorder of country life as well. In the last few years of his brief life, however, there matured in Jefferies a deepened response to the physical world. The transformation is evident in his late essays, which reveal him to have a sense of wonder about his surroundings that is markedly different from Gilbert White's. This response of course reflects his participation in the romantic attitude toward nature best exemplified in English literature by Wordsworth, yet Jefferies' pages show that what he has to say is profoundly rooted in his own experience.

In one of his works, not published until sixty years after his death, he goes back in memory to the old farm at Coate where he lived as a boy, recalling how on dewless summer nights he lay on the grass footpath. "Looking straight up . . . from the path to the stars," he writes, "it was clear and evident that I was really riding among them; they were not above, nor all round, but I was in the midst of them." If true at night, it was also true of the day despite the obscuring sunlight. As he puts it, "I walked amongst the stars. I had not got then to leave this world to enter space: I was already there. The vision is indeed contracted, nor can we lift our feet further than the earth; yet we are really among these things to-day. The eye sees further at night than at noon."

Seeing in this way, Jefferies did not feel himself to be so much an individual as he did part of a universal whole. His sense of where he was, in other words, expanded from his spot of earth in Wiltshire to assume cosmic dimensions. And in this context nature became miraculous, as is exemplified in the following description of a numinous moment:

> I went to drink at the spring: the clear, cool, and sweet water tempted me in the summer. Stooping in the rocky cell, I lifted the water in the hollow of my hand, carefully else the sand might be disturbed. The sunlight gleamed on it as it slipped through my fingers; thus I had the sun, too, in my palm. Alone, under the roots of the trees and the step stone; alone, with the sunlight and the pure water, there was a sense of something more than these; the water was more to me than water; and the sun than sun—as if I had something in common with them and could feel with them. The gleaming ray on the liquid in my palm held me in its possession for the moment: the touch of the water gave me something from itself; it dropped from my fingers and

> was gone; the gleam disappeared, but I had had them. Beside the physical water and the physical light, my soul had received from them their beauty.

Like Eiseley in *The Immense Journey*, Jefferies here reports from his own wilderness, sharing with us something of the marvels to be experienced there. This is just what the literary naturalist is especially qualified to do. Because, as Eiseley writes, we customarily "rush to and fro like Mad Hatters upon our peculiar errands, all the time imagining our surroundings to be dull and ourselves quite ordinary creatures," we occasionally find it necessary to "send emissaries into the wilderness in the hope of learning of great events . . . that will resuscitate [our] waning taste for life." Jefferies was an Ishmael figure of this sort, one of those who sought "what only the solitary approach can give—a natural revelation" (*IJ*, 164).

Given this outlook on his part, we can well understand why Jefferies would say, "Let us not be too entirely mechanical, Baconian, and experimental only." He does not deny the value of knowledge gained by such means, but, anticipating Eiseley's remarks in "The Enchanted Glass," he finds it far too limited in scope. "Man's mind is the most important fact with which we are yet acquainted," he declares. "Let us not turn then against it and deny its existence with too many brazen instruments." Instead he advocates the further use of the mind to understand what is "*symbolized* by the leaf, the flower, the very touch of earth" (my emphasis). In the marvelous world he evokes there are many mysteries, mysteries we are given the opportunity to search out. And in this search nothing must be neglected or overlooked—"not so much as a fallen leaf or a grain of sand. Literally everything bears stamped upon it characters in the hieratic, the sacred handwriting, not one word of which shall fall to the ground."

This last is a key sentence in Jefferies' writings, which makes clear a close kinship with his American contemporary, Thoreau, as well as with Eiseley, his descendent in the literary-naturalist tradition. Before considering the matter of natural hieroglyphics, however, we need to take into account the place of W. H. Hudson in this tradition. He is important, in part, because he is the only one of Eiseley's four named predecessors to have reported from a literal wilderness. His "parish of Selborne," as he calls it, was the 200,000 square miles of pampean country in Argentina. Although he had already been living in England for over twenty years when *The Naturalist in La Plata* was published in 1892, the wild region of his childhood and youth was still very much with him. He too had looked closely about him and was able to describe his surroundings in engaging detail. But instead of swallows and buttercups, what he saw was the pervasive pampa grass, "the spears of which often attain a height of eight or nine feet," and such creatures as the puma, the crested screamer, the rhea, and the vizcacha. In his writing Hudson celebrates this wilderness area "where no lines of house or hedge mar the enchanting disorder of nature."

Since he was a native of the wild, so to speak, Hudson's world inevitably contrasts with White's and Jefferies' alike. Yet, being a romantic, he has much closer affinities with the man from Coate than he does with the Selborne parson. Reminding us of Jefferies at the spring, Hudson acknowledges experiencing "special moments" in the natural world, moments that carried with them a "special grace." Elsewhere he offers this explanation for such experiences:

> We may say that impressions are vivid and live vividly in the mind, even to the end of life, in those alone in whom something that is of the child survives in the adult—the measureless delight in all this visible world. . . ; and, with the delight, the sense of wonder in all life, which is akin to, if not one with, the mythical faculty, and if experienced in a high degree is a sense of the supernatural in all natural things.

Thus, although Hudson was widely read in the scientific literature of his day, his temperament prompted him to second Jefferies in his distrust of the objective methods of purely scientific inquiry. Sounding much more like a poet than a scientist, more a Whitman than a Darwin, he wrote that "unless the soul goes out to meet what we see we do not see it; nothing do we see, not a beetle, not a blade of grass."

If Richard Jefferies' sense of wonder about the natural world can be said to pass beyond that expressed by Gilbert White, then Hudson's response can in a similar fashion be seen to exceed Jefferies'. For Hudson evoked not only the wonder but also the terror of existence, with the latter stemming from his consciousness of death both as an individual inevitability and as a universal fact. In one place he writes, "Death is a reality only when it is very near, so close on us that we can actually hear its swift stoaty feet rustling over the dead leaves, and for a brief bitter space we actually know that his sharp teeth will presently be in our throat." The dread caused by the image of death-as-predator became mixed with horror as well when he considered the practices of certain creatures that, from a human point of view, seem uncommonly cruel. (Especially repugnant to him were wasps and ichneumon flies, who paralyze their prey so that their young may devour live food.) Finally there was his awareness of the staggering wastefulness of nature: first in the extinction of entire species; and second in the massive destruction wrought by unpredictable catastrophes such as floods, droughts, and plagues. This knowledge could produce in him a mood of metaphysical fright, prompting such a comment as this (following the bird massacre caused by a great frost in Cornwall): "[T]he darkest imaginings of men—the blackest phantom or image of himself which he has sacrificed to—was not so dark as this dreadful unintelligible and unintelligent power that made us, in which we live and move and have our being."

This passage reveals a striking connection between Hudson and Melville's fictional character who, presumably speaking for the author himself, observes, "Though in many of its aspects the visible world seems formed in love, the invisible spheres were formed in fright." And both show their kinship with Eiseley, who increasingly saw the natural world as terrifying rather than as benignly marvelous. Even at the end of *The Immense Journey*, the sunniest of his books, he comments, "I am sure now that life is not what it is purported to be and that nature, in the canny words of a Scotch theologue, 'is not as natural as it looks' " (*IJ*, 197). And the darker view that characterizes most of his subsequent work finds memorable expression in his recognition that "behind visible nature lurks an invisible and procreant void from whose incomprehensible magnitude we can only recoil" (*UU*, 31). For this twentieth-century Ishmael the essentially optimistic outlook of Jefferies could not long be sustained.

H. D. Thoreau, Jefferies' younger American contemporary, is also remembered as one with a hopeful, forward-looking approach to life. That is because in *Walden*, presenting himself as a celebrator of morning and spring, he succeeded in creating "a vast rebirth ritual, the purest and most complete in our literature." It may therefore seem unlikely that Eiseley, noted for his fascination with night and autumn, should be attracted to his East Coast forebear in the literary-naturalist tradition. Yet there are more similarities between the two of them than first meet the eye.

Eiseley himself was aware that Thoreau has proven to be an elusive, perplexing figure, one who strikes different people in very different ways. Noting in one of his essays the uncertainty with which Thoreau continues to be viewed, Eiseley calls him "a fox at the wood's edge, regarding human preoccupations with doubt" (*ST*, 224). These words make evident one sense in which the native Nebraskan felt an affinity with the man from Concord, because in other contexts Eiseley refers to himself in similar fashion. At the beginning of *The Night Country*, for instance, he writes, "The fact that I wear the protective coloration of sedate citizenship is a ruse of the fox—I learned it long ago. The facts of my inner life are quite otherwise" (*NC*, 4).

In another essay, still pursuing Thoreau's enigmatic quality, he quotes some well-known comments that Ellery Channing made about his friend: "I have never been able to understand what he meant by his life. Why was he so interested in the river and the woods. . . ? Something peculiar here I judge" (*ST*, 235). Likewise we might judge that there was something peculiar about Eiseley. Why did he pay so little attention to other people in his writings? Why was he so interested in bleak uplands and the remains of creatures long dead? What did he mean by *his* life? Clearly Eiseley was drawn to Thoreau because he felt in him a kindred spirit.

Perhaps we can best approach their kinship by first considering a comment once made by Rachel Carson. "If I had the influence with the good fairy who is supposed to preside over the christening of all children," she writes, "I should ask that her gift to each child in the world would be a sense of wonder so indestructible that it would last throughout life, as an unfailing antidote against the boredom and disenchantments of later years, the sterile preoccupation with things that are artficial, the alienation from the sources of our strength." It is this sense of wonder, founded in an awareness of the ultimate mystery of creation, that all the great contemplative naturalists did in fact retain throughout their lives. One finds some evidence of it even in Gilbert White, who wrote in his preface, "If the writer should at all appear to have induced any of his readers to pay a more ready attention to the wonders of Creation, too frequently overlooked as common occurrences . . . , his purpose will be fully answered." Yet it is much more apparent in the works of those writers influenced by the revolution in sensibility that goes by the name of romanticism.

The book of nature had of course been read for centuries before the romantics came along. But in Christian tradition it was always contrasted with the Bible, the book of divine revelation. This book was inevitably the more highly valued of the two, because it was understood to be the source of all supernatural knowledge, of all that was necessary for the health of the soul. The efficacy of the other book, the one whose pages lay open for all to see, was far less certain. At best it could lead only to as much appreciation or understanding of its Author as varying individual sense impressions (combined with reason) would allow. At worst, being in a corrupt state ever since the Fall, it could lead to the destruction of the soul by tempting one to delight in the senses for their own sakes.

Milton suggests the predicament at the end of his epic fable. There he presents us with the stark spectacle of two figures, Man and Woman, who "with wandering steps and slow . . . took their solitary way" into the world that now lay before them. It is a prototypical scene in literature, which captures in unforgettable fashion a universal aspect of the human condition. But this moment of loneliness and uncertainty is not without hope, for the archangel

Michael mentions to Adam the possibility of possessing within himself a paradise "happier far" than the one he has just lost.

It took an admirer of Milton, however, a poet who came later and broke away from doctrinal Christianity, to show (rather than merely proclaim) a way in which this opportunity might be realized. Driven by an inner necessity, Wordsworth convincingly demonstrated how the supernatural of religious tradition could be found by the ardent seeker in the very heart of the natural. He succeeded, in other words, in delineating a paradise that "can be achieved simply by a union of man's mind with nature, and so is a present paradise in this world." It was a momentous accomplishment, one which changed forever the way we perceive our natural surroundings.

All three of the nineteenth-century naturalists mentioned earlier reflect this change in their work. Hudson acknowledges it in his reference to outdoor moments of special grace, and Jefferies gives a lyrical account of one such moment in his experience at the spring. A champion of alertness, Thoreau makes even clearer the connection between the natural and the transcendental in the following passage from *Walden*: "Men esteem truth remote, in the outskirts of the system, behind the farthest star, before Adam and after the last man. In eternity there is indeed something true and sublime. But all these times and places and occasions are now and here. God himself culminates in the present moment, and will never be more divine in the lapse of all the ages." For Thoreau the present is holy ground because he has learned how to see signs of the eternal in all the particulars of the natural world.

Despite Jefferies' assertion that no word of the hieratic handwriting shall fall to the dust, it is obvious that not everyone is equally adept at reading nature's book. It often seems obscure, difficult to decipher, as though the alphabet used were unfamiliar. This is at least partly because the attentiveness required to really look at what is always before us is not easy to maintain.

Thoreau was a master of this discipline, however, and in the following account in *Walden* of a thawing sandy bank he provides a remarkable example of his method of nature reading:

> Innumerable little streams overlap and interlace with one another, exhibiting a sort of hybrid product, which obeys half way the law of currents, and half way that of vegetation. As it flows it takes the forms of sappy leaves or vines, making heaps of pulpy sprays a foot or more in depth, and resembling, as you look down on them, the laciniated lobed and imbricated thalluses of some lichens; or you are reminded of coral, of leopards' paws or birds' feet, of brains or lungs or bowels, and excrements of all kinds.

Among all these carefully observed animal and vegetable shapes, it is the leaf forms that most impress Thoreau, leading him to conclude that "[t]he Maker of this earth but patented a leaf," from which has followed all of the operations in nature. "What Champollion will decipher this hieroglyphic for us," he asks, "that we may turn over a new leaf at last?"

The answer is provided by Thoreau himself, who declares in four unambiguous words what he has learned from his close reading: "There is nothing inorganic." He has beheld with wonder-filled eyes "not a fossil earth, but a living earth," and faith in the possibilities of restoration in human life is a consequence of his vision. Who has need of a foreign decipherer? Thoreau is his own Champollion.

So, too, is Eiseley. In his very first collection of connected essays he makes it clear that he is one of those Ishmael figures who seeks "a natural revelation" through the solitary exploration of his surroundings (*IJ*, 164). "My album is the earth," he asserts elsewhere (*NC*, 161), and much of his writing consists of an attempt to interpret the hieroglyphics contained in that book.

One example of his reading is provided by an experience he had while walking along the shore of a desolate island off the Gulf Coast. "I caught a glimpse of a beautiful shell," he writes, "imprinted with what appeared to be strange writing, rolling in the breakers. Impelled by curiosity, I leaped into the surf and salvaged it. Golden characters like Chinese hieroglyphs ran in symmetrical lines around the cone of the shell. I lifted it up with the utmost excitement, as though a message had come to me from the green depths of the sea" (*UU*, 145). Later, after it was identified as a *Conus spurious atlanticus*, or alphabet shell, Eiseley left with his find and subsequently placed it upon his desk. Handling it as reverently as he would the tablets of a lost civilization, he says he probably would not have had "so complete a revelation" if the shell had not been misnamed *Conus spurious* by someone who had misread "a true message from the universe." True because the shell, in epiphanic fashion, prompts Eiseley to see that "the golden alphabet, in whatever shape it chooses to reveal itself, is never spurious. From its inscrutable lettering is created man and all the streaming cloudland of his dreams" (*UU*, 146).

As this passage and the one from *Walden* show, a natural fact often does not remain simply a fact for Eiseley and Thoreau. They perceive it as having symbolic significance, as somehow conveying hidden truths, even as being miraculous. Indeed, their primary function as contemplative naturalists is to see more deeply into nature, to make more connections than the rest of us, and to bring what they have discovered back to the human community.

The motivating force behind this endeavor—both the forays of certain individuals into the wilderness and the listening of the rest of us to their words—is the yearning for significance. It is a universal longing, memorably evoked by Eiseley in the following passage:

> Since man first saw an impossible visage staring upward from a still pool, he has been haunted by meanings—meanings felt even in the wood, where the trees leaned over him, manifesting a vast and living presence. The image in the pool vanished at the touch of his finger, but he went home and created a legend. The great trees never spoke, but man knew that dryads slipped among their boles. Since the red morning of time it has been so, and the compulsive reading of such manuscripts will continue to occupy man's attention long after the books that contain his inmost thoughts have been sealed away by the indefatigable spider (*UU*, 194).

Yet, as Eiseley is also aware, "Each man deciphers from the ancient alphabet of nature only those secrets that his own deeps possess the power to endow with meaning" (*UU*, 146). What is perceived, in other words, depends primarily on the character of the perceiver, and once we acknowledge this fact we are bound to observe significant differences between Eiseley and Thoreau.

In part these differences are the result of marked changes in our cultural climate. Thoreau, after all, is a representative of pre-Civil War America, and despite the sharp criticism he has to offer of nineteenth-century materialism, his vision remains essentially youthful and forward looking. Thus, even though recent commentators have emphasized the dark, troubled aspects of his life and character, the dominant mood of *Walden*, the work that has chiefly earned him his place in the American pantheon, is sanguine. And in the essay entitled "Walking" (or "The Wild"), he tells of heading always in a westerly direction on his rambles, a habit he relates to the westering of the nation and of civilization as a whole. Moving west therefore suggests youthful energy, hopefulness, freshness, vigor. In his quiet way Thoreau has links to Whitman, who more boisterously celebrated the possibilities of the young nation while singing a song of himself. It is this spirit in Thoreau that helps make him a romantic.

Eiseley, on the other hand, is a twentieth-century figure who grew up in the West that Thoreau had only read or heard about. By his time there was no symbolic reason for heading further in the direction of the Pacific, and those who did so when he was a young man in the thirties were primarily driven by desperation, not hope. This transformation in the national spirit is reflected in Eiseley's voice from the very beginning. Like T. S. Eliot, his older midcountry contemporary, he never sounds young, as is suggested by the mere titles of some of the poems written during his undergraduate years: "For a Lost Home," "Nocturne for Autumn's Ending," "Sonnet for Age," "The Quainter Dust," "Now the Singing Is Done." Perhaps the tone of this early verse is best captured in a few lines from "Spiders," first published when he was only twenty:

> Spiders are old—
> they watch from dark corners while wills are made.
> They leave grey webs for flies, and wait . . .
> tiles drop from the roof,
> leaves turn moldy under the black, slanting rain,
> people die . . .
> and the spiders inherit everything (*ANW*, 3).

This is romantic also, but not in a Thoreauvian key. Youthful idealism has been replaced by *Weltschmerz*, by images of aging, decay, and death.

Striking differences likewise appear when we consider the specific answer each gives to the key question of place. Thoreau, of course, has become permanently associated with Walden Pond. One of its most salient characteristics is that its scenery is "on a humble scale," beautiful but without grandeur. With a circumference of only a mile and three quarters, the clear deep pond is completely encompassed by woodland, rising "by just gradations from the low shrubs of the shore to the highest trees" of the surrounding hills. This enclosed landscape seems to provide a sense of security or protection, which may be what prompts Thoreau to see the pond in human or, more specifically, feminine terms. In one passage he writes that "of all the characters I have known, perhaps Walden wears best, and best preserves its purity." Elsewhere he refers to it "throwing off its nightly clothing of mist," and to "the gentle pulsing of its life, the heaving of its breast." In this environment Thoreau is moved to extol "[t]he indescribable innocence and beneficence of Nature," and to declare, "There can be no very black melancholy to him who lives in the midst of Nature and has his senses still."

The famous Walden setting exemplifies what theorists a century before Thoreau would have called the beautiful. As summarized by M. H. Abrams, this aesthetic category refers to a natural scene that "is small in scale, orderly, and tranquil, effects pleasure on the observer, and is associated with love." Such a landscape was ideally suited to the New Englander, whose personal background was so contrary to Eiseley's. Having spent a secure childhood in the company of his parents, two sisters, and a brother, Thoreau had a strongly developed home sense, which extended beyond his immediate family to the town of Concord, as is revealed by his unwillingness to leave and his homesickness when away. For all intents and purposes, in fact, he never left the town, and he died in the house where his father died before him and his mother still lived.

Nietzsche says somewhere that all landscapes are symbolic. Certainly this is true of Walden, which, as Thoreau presents it, is more expressive of his inner spirit than it is a description of the external world. One can confirm this simply by paying a visit to what is, after all, a very ordinary small woodland lake. Walden is primarily a state of mind, one that was alien to Eiseley and that he consequently never describes as a physical reality. Instead, given his very different early experiences, the natural setting that became indelibly fixed in his mind—the one he kept returning to in imagination long after he left it in body—is the Badlands.

Characterized by high pinnacle rocks and deep gullies, this vast arid territory is, according to Eiseley, a wasteland "as lifeless as that valley in which lie the kings of Egypt," a place where no vegetation grows and the only shade to be found is beneath the toadstool shapes of windswept sandstone (*IJ*, 170). In this inhuman landscape nature shows no signs of beneficence, and it is easy to understand how anyone who has his senses could succumb to melancholy while in the midst of it. Once ruled by great beasts who "never had the misfortune to look upon a human face" (*ASH*, 87), it now "has silences as deep as those in the moon's airless chasms" (*IJ*, 170). Furthermore, as Eiseley observes, "Everything is flaking, cracking, disintegrating, wearing away in the long, imperceptible weather of time . . . , and [the] colors in that waste are the colors that flame in the lonely sunsets on dead planets" (*IJ*, 170).

No European theorists of the eighteenth century would have come upon such a prospect, yet it is a desiccated version of the sublime, the other side of their aesthetic dichotomy. A setting of this sort, as Abrams explains, "is vast (hence suggestive of infinity), wild, tumultuous and awful, is associated with pain, and evokes ambivalent feelings of terror and admiration." Once again we grasp the symbolic dimension of the landscape. Like Walden the Badlands can be visited, but Eiseley's description makes us aware of the extent to which what he saw there was emblematic of the geography of his spirit. In his autobiography he admits that the place enthralled him, that his recall of the time he spent there was almost eidetic, and that much of what "seared its way into [his] brain and into [his] writing" had its origin in that desolate region (*ASH*, 87).

Only once, to my knowledge, did Thoreau confront nature in

its sublime aspect. Described in *The Maine Woods*, the experience occurred when he reached the summit of Mount Katahdin. Stumbling on naked rocks among the clouds, he found the spot savage and titanic, alien to man. "It was Matter, vast, teriffic—not his Mother Earth that we have heard of, not for him to trod on, or be buried in. . . . There was clearly felt the presence of a force not bound to be kind to man." Shaken by the encounter, Thoreau exclaims, "I stand in awe of my body, this matter to which I am bound has become so strange to me. . . . Talk of mysteries! . . . *Who* are we? *where* are we?" Such a mood is exceptional in Thoreau, but is a leitmotif in the works of Eiseley, a man on whom nature rarely seems to have shown her smiling face.

Where are we? In the context presented above the question does more than anticipate one of Heard's, because we know it cannot be answered scientifically. Detailed observations and exact measurements, such as Thoreau himself made of Walden Pond, will not serve the purpose here. What he wants to know is akin to what the child is after when he asks where he came from. It is an essentially religious question, and a naturalistic answer will not satisfy the inquirer's curiosity.

Eiseley's own attempts to answer the question lead him to consider the concept of nature itself. He is of course aware that it is an extremely problematical abstraction, one that has been defined in many different ways throughout the centuries of recorded history. In his own view the word "implies all, absolutely all, that man knows or can know" (*ST*, 226). It is the concept that lurks behind all religions, he writes, being equally evident "in the burial cults of Neanderthal man, in Cro-Magnon hunting art, in the questions of Job and in the answering voice from the whirlwind" (*ST*, 225). It is an enduring reality, as the creature called man has apparently always known, one that both precedes our individual births and persists after our individual deaths. Thus, Eiseley declares, "Nature remains an otherness which incorporates man, but which man instinctively feels contains secrets denied to him" (*ST*, 225).

Yet he does not remain long in the realm of theoretical speculation. On the contrary he helps us *feel* the notion of otherness by relating an anecdote from his childhood about a huge tropical shell that his aunt kept on her inland dressing table. What wandering relative had brought her the iridescent shell he does not know, but he remembers it being held up to his ear:

> Out of the great shell, even in that silent bedroom, I, who had never seen the ocean, heard the whispered sibilance, the sigh of waves upon the beach, the little murmurs of moving water, the confused mewing of gulls in the sun-bright air. It was my first miracle, indeed perhaps my first awareness of the otherness of nature, of myself outside, in a sense, and listening, as though beyond light-years to a remote event. Perhaps, in that Victorian bedroom with its knickknacks and curios, I had suddenly fallen out of the nature I inhabited and turned, for the first time, to survey her with surprise (*ST*, 217).

Nor does it matter, he goes on to say, that during his college years he discovered what he really heard were the magnified sounds of his own blood and of the house around him. The sense of otherness still remained.

For the boy that otherness was marvelous, and the adult Eiseley never lost his childhood sense of it. In this connection we may recall his memory of the multitude of brown birds who, in the roadside hedge near the bishop's house, waited out a storm in a silence "so secret and immense" that he was awestruck. A similar feeling characterizes Eiseley's response even to such a process as photosynthesis. He reminds us that until our lifeless planet produced green leaves that in turn altered the chemical complexion of the atmosphere, animal forms could not have arisen out of previously inert matter. "Only after long observation does the sophisticated eye succeed in labeling these events as natural rather than miraculous," he writes. "There frequently lingers about them a penumbral air of mystery not easily dispersed" (*UU*, 97).

Although Eiseley came to believe that "in the world there is nothing to explain the world" (*ASH*, 245), much of his work consists of attempts to understand nature. But, given his temperament and the changes wrought in the twentieth century, "the one great hieroglyph" (*ST*, 237) did not yield the same kind of meanings to him as it did to Jefferies and Thoreau. Eiseley could never forget the void out of which the world emerged, nor that the earth itself "contains . . . the dark heart of nothingness, from which springs all that lives" (*UU*,148).

In his efforts to plumb the great mystery, he therefore most characteristically focuses on its shadowy rather than its luminous manifestations. It is not enough for him to mention, for instance, that *Homo sapiens* emerged during the Pleistocene period. Instead he elaborates on this straightforward statement by emphasizing that it was an age of great extinctions, when perhaps seventy per cent of the animal life in the Western world perished (*UU*,119). The implication here is that mankind, by a trick of nature, was in some way foredoomed by its ice-age origin.

But Eiseley did not have to reach back into the geological past in order to find ominous signs of the mysteriousness of nature. He could discover ample evidence in his own suburban neighborhood, as is shown by his meditations on the Sphex wasps who one autumn burrowed into the backyard of the apartment house where he lived. These wasps are giants of their kind—a neighbor even thought the tunnelings in the lawn must have been made by moles—and are one of the species whose habits were so repugnant to W. H. Hudson.

Eiseley finds these tiger-faced wasps beautiful in the sunlight, yet he too feels the terror that their behavior can arouse. Relying in large part on the observations of the great French naturalist Henri Fabre, he writes,

> The fearsome operations of these wasps depend upon an uncanny knowledge of the location of the nerve centers of their prey in order to stun, not kill the creature. The larvae, also, must possess an instinctive knowledge of how to eat in order to prolong the life of the paralyzed body which they devour. To complicate matters further, the victim . . . seems to have some foreknowledge of its helplessness, some fear of which its agile opponent takes absolute confident advantage (*ASH*, 247–248).

Eiseley is an evolutionist and believes that the Sphexes have evolved in the manner of other creatures, but he is admittedly baffled by the instincts revealed here. Echoing questions raised by Darwin as well as Fabre, he wonders how the pure chance of natural selection could have produced the complicated interlocking behaviors of the adult insect and its larvae. Or, on the other hand, if he suspends disbelief and grants that somehow in fact it did, he then is led to ask why the same force wouldn't also have led the cicada to develop a defense against its enemy.

A Sphex assassin may never accidentally have bumped into one of *our* noses, and we may not be aware of ever having heard "an occasional cicada's song terminating abruptly in a kind of stifled shriek" (*ASH*, 243), but Eiseley's discussion is authoritative and convincing. By acquainting ourselves with it we come to a better understanding of its author's awe before the mystery of life and are prompted to feel a heightened sense of that mysteriousness ourselves. Eiseley's readings in the book of nature, in other words, help us to see the world through his eyes. If so, then he has successfully performed in his individual way the chief function of all the contemplative naturalists we have considered.

Yet the aspect of the natural world Eiseley has made most distinctively his own, the one with which he deals more extensively than all his predecessors combined, has still to be considered. It is the phenomenon of time. In the opening chapter of his very first book he admits to being preoccupied with this dimension of our human awareness of the world (*IJ*, 12-13), and in subsequent books his preoccupation becomes increasingly apparent.

"Time is but the stream I go a-fishing in," Thoreau declares in one of the better known passages of *Walden*. Such a nonchalant sentence—whatever the unexpressed disappointments, frustrations, and anxieties of the man who wrote it—could never have come from Eiseley's time-harried pen. In calling to mind the period of man's emergence, for instance, he speaks of the development of a layer of "crystalline thought substance" in the human brain that superseded "the dark, forgetful pathways of the animal brain." As a result, he observes, "There was no longer a single generation, which bred blindly and without question. Time and its agonizing nostalgia would touch the heart each season and be seen in the fall of a leaf" (*UU*, 104). Certainly Eiseley himself was profoundly touched. As he writes in another place, "My sense of time is so heightened that I can feel the frost at work in the stones, the first creeping advance of grass in a deserted street" (*NC*, 158).

Time is different from other aspects of the world dealt with by our writer-naturalists in that it cannot be directly apprehended by the senses. Instead it is reflected in the movement of, or change in, tangible physical phenomena. Because this is so, time has been conceptualized in different ways by people in different periods and places. Eiseley's interest in this cultural variation is limited to the Western tradition, especially in the development of the classical, Christian, and evolutionary concepts of time.

Conceiving of time as cyclical, the ancient world was "bound to the wheel of Ixion, to the maxim: what has been is, passes, and will be" (*NC*, 64). But the triumph of Christianity brought about a radical break with the pagan past. Time, now rooted in the drama of the Fall and the Redemption, became unreturning and irreversible. "Novelty was its essence," Eiseley writes, "just as duration and repetition lay at the heart of classical thinking" (*NC*, 64).

The Christian view dominated Western thought for close to two thousand years. During the last century, however, scientific discoveries have resulted in still another radical shift in the notion of time, albeit one that incorporates elements from both of the earlier conceptions. As advances in geology and biology have proved beyond all doubt, evolutionary time is vast in scale, extraordinarily more extensive than the few millennia to which the Christian notion was restricted. To this extent, then, the intuition of the ancients has been vindicated. Yet in ways inconceivable to the biblical writers or the fathers of the Church, scientists have also demonstrated that time is in fact unrepeatable. The concept of evolutionary time thus retains the idea of a great play, but the performance turns out to have become increasingly unpredictable and mysterious. As if still anticipating the shift in outlook, Eiseley characterizes it in the following way:

> The tragedy on a barren hill in Judea, which for so long had held human attention, would seem to shrink to a miniscule event on a sand-

> grain planet lost in a whirl of fiery galaxies. Reluctantly men would peer into the hollow eye sockets of the beasts from which they had sprung. The Christian dream would linger but the surety of direction would depart. Nature, the second book of the theologians, would prove even more difficult of interpretation than the first (*NC*, 68).

Eiseley is of course intellectually committed to the concept of evolutionary time. Yet one of his great merits as a literary naturalist is the way his readings in nature's book help us to feel the concept, to grasp it at some level other than the rational. Eiseley himself evidently arrived at this deepened understanding as a result of his bone-hunting days in western Nebraska.

The most dramatic experience he relates concerns the discovery of a fossil quarry, a site to which he and some companions were taken by an old man who had stumbled upon the place twenty years earlier. Pa Mullens, Eiseley's fictional name for the real-life George Bennet, belonged to a fundamentalist sect that "lent no credence to modern geological heresies," and he told the university men how all the bones he had seen must have been "the garbage from the biggest Flood of all . . . come right down to our valley" (*NC*, 120). Although this recitation was not encouraging to Eiseley and the others, the old man did have in his possession a huge brown thigh bone that they recognized as belonging to some long-vanished species of mammoth or mastodon. Thus they let Mullens lead them on, hoping that he would remember where he had found the bone.

First they traveled across the prairie by car from Mullens's house to a barrier of stony hills. Next they went on foot, climbing over one barren hill after another, until at long last the wheezing and choking old man let out an exclamation. Then Eiseley writes:

> There was a late afternoon sun playing on that hillside, and I can remember still the way my eyes traveled down it from boulder to gray boulder between the spines of Spanish bayonet. And then I saw it. Maybe this won't mean anything to you. Maybe you don't understand this game, or why men follow it. But I saw it. I tell you I saw five million years of the planet's history lying there on that hillside with the yucca growing over it and the roots working through it, just the way the old man had remembered it from a day long ago in the sun.
>
> I saw the ivory from the tusks of elephants scattered like broken

> china that the rain has washed. I saw the splintered, mineralized enamel of huge unknown teeth. I paused over the bones of ferocious bear-dog carnivores. I saw, protruding from an eroding gully, the jaw of a shovel-tusked amebelodont that has been gone twice a million years into the night of geologic time. I tell you I saw it with my own eyes and I knew, even as I looked at it, that I would never see anything like it again (*NC*, 121–22).

Old man Mullens may have lived in "a small, tight world of marvels" with his literal belief in Noah and the Flood (*NC*, 123), but Eiseley's presentation here shows that in a different way the discovery of the quarry was at least as marvelous to him. Previous to this he had read about the theory of evolution. Now, in the form of innumerable fossils that could be seen and touched, he was confronted with overwhelming evidence of the truth of what he had learned from books. The episode reads almost like the account of a conversion. No longer simply a concept, evolutionary time becomes a felt reality in this story.

Eiseley's unusual time-consciousness is revealed in a more reflective way in two other extended passages, the first of which occupies most of the introductory chapter of *The Immense Journey*. There Eiseley depicts himself riding across a sunlit prairie until, stopped by "a great wall of naked sandstone and clay," he comes upon "the Slit" (*IJ*, 3). It is a crack of about body width in the earth, and he works his way into it in search of fossils. As he slides downward, further and further from the light, he finds a prehuman skull embedded in the sandstone wall. Ashen and waterworn, this skull becomes the occasion for the meditations that occupy much of the rest of the essay.

Although Eiseley's thoughts range far and wide, he keeps returning to the theme of time. First he recognizes that the skull came from early on in the age of mammals, from "far back along those converging roads where . . . cat and man and weasel must leap into a single shape" (*IJ*, 5). From that focal point he then moves backward and forward in his mind, and is thereby led to consider his own place in the scheme of things. "The creature had never lived to see a man," he writes, "and I, what was I never going to see?" (*IJ*,

5). He realizes that he is caught on a pinpoint of evolutionary time. With his scientific knowledge he can exercise his imagination in order to look backward, but he is ignorant of the future, from which perspective he is himself already a fossil.

As Professor Carlisle has previously observed, the consistent capitalization of the word *Slit* helps us to understand that more is involved here than simple fossil excavation. And Eiseley himself points out that the Slit had come to symbolize in his mind "a dimension denied to man, the dimension of time" (*IJ*, 11). Following up this idea in a later work, he refers to "the wound of time," which is caused by the ability of the human mind "to extend itself across a duration greater than the capacity of mortal flesh to endure" (*NC*, 221). What does it all mean? "Down how many roads among the stars must man propel himself in search of the final secret?" (*IJ*, 12). In pondering this question in *The Immense Journey*, Eiseley conjectures that there may be no meaning "save that of the journey itself" (*IJ*, 6). Yet perhaps that is reason enough, he suggests, because "the changes brought us here," and it has been "a good journey under a pleasant sun" (*IJ*, 6–7).

In none of his subsequent works, however, does Eiseley treat the matter of time with such apparent equanimity. Indeed, in a book published only three years after *The Immense Journey*, we find a markedly different response to a similar experience. Once again alone on horseback, he rides to the top of a mountain, but on this occasion, as he frankly admits, he was "surfeited with the smell of mortality" (*FT*, 160). Consequently, although nothing moved as he picked his way through boulder fields, he could still "feel time like an enemy behind each stone" (*FT*, 161).

Next he recounts his ride into the canyon on the far side of the mountain. As with his climb downward inside the Slit, this descent also becomes a brief trip through time as well as space. Combining the eye of a scientist who can recognize the signs of different evolutionary eras, and the voice of a poet who is able to make them vivid, Eiseley presents his ride as "a journey into the eons of the past" (*FT*, 163). And when he at last reins up on the arid, sandy floor of the canyon, he feels as though he had gone down to the end—"to the place of fires where we first began" (*FT*, 164).

Then, letting his gaze rise gradually from its present depth to the slopes at the top of the mountain, he thinks about the slow, tremendously extended journey of animal life up that same road. "I had come down the whole way," he realizes, "into a place where one could lift sand and ask in a hollow, dust-shrouded whisper, 'Life, what is it? Why am I here? Why am I here?' " (*FT*, 165). Yet no voice responds from the whirlwind of his distracted mind, and the sky remains mute. There are no answers to the questions he is impelled to ask, the immemorial questions of a time-haunted creature who finds himself abandoned in a place that provides no satisfying explanations of its own inscrutability. As he comments, "The living river flowed out of nowhere into nothing. No one knew its source or its departing" (*FT*, 165).

For Eiseley, as for the romantic writers he admired, nature is revelatory. But even adepts in reading nature's book—those who find their true vocation in deciphering its hieroglyphics—do not have the same meanings revealed to them. At least in part Eiseley's uniqueness is a product of his having been frightened by time. We know that he is the sort of man who has "lain awake and grasped the sides of a cot, staring upward into the dark while the slow clock strokes begin" (*FT*, 167). And it is this experience of dread, in turn, that helps him to translate the mute language of stones and bones in a way that evokes a kind of religious awe before the mysteries of the universe.

Such feeling is characteristic of romantic nature writing. In fact, for all of Eiseley's predecessors in this tradition the wilderness was in some sense holy. Thoreau is even reported to have announced, when asked about his unwillingness to attend church, that he worshipped outdoors. Eiseley cannot properly be said to have done that, but he did have a disposition that in its idiosyncratic way was unmistakably religious. Part and parcel of the Ishmaelian sensibility that permeates his work, this aspect of his temperament now needs to be given close consideration.

IV

The Uses of Loneliness

> Remembering speechlessly we seek the great forgotten language, the lost lane-end into heaven, a stone, a leaf, an unfound door. Where? When? O lost, and by the wind grieved, ghost come back again.
>
> —Thomas Wolfe

In *The Sacred and the Profane* Mircea Eliade distinguishes between religious man and the man without religious feeling. He describes the latter, a product of modern industrialized society, as one "who lives, or wishes to live, in a desacralized world." A famous example of such a man is Sigmund Freud. Although not mentioned by Eliade in this regard, Freud is in the forefront of those modern thinkers who helped develop the idea of a wholly profane world. His outlook is made evident at the beginning of *Civilization and Its Discontents*, where he mentions Romain Rolland's view that religious sentiments have their source in a feeling of "something limitless, unbounded—as it were, 'oceanic.' " Freud was willing to grant the existence of this feeling in others, but he saw it as a survival of "an early phase of ego-feeling," one that ideally should be outgrown in the adult. In any case, tracing the origin of the religious attitude back to infantile helplessness, Freud rejected Rolland's view and flatly declared, "I cannot discover this 'oceanic' feeling in myself."

Although trained as a scientist and necessarily a citizen of the modern world, Loren Eiseley is temperamentally far removed from the founder of psychoanalysis. In "Science and the Sense of the Holy" he refers to this same passage from Freud's book only to criticize it (*ST*, 186–91), and in his autobiography he frankly acknowledges that his whole life has been "a religious pilgrimage" despite his lack of adherence to any church or formal creed (*ASH*, 146). Even more revealing, however, are the various signs of *Homo religiosus* that are woven into the very fabric of his essays. Eliade observes that nature for religious man "is never only 'natural'; it is always fraught with religious value." Certainly this is true of Eiseley. As the last chapter has shown, his deciphering of nature's hieroglyphics reveals his penchant for finding transcendental significance in concrete earthly phenomena, and his confrontation with time carries with it some of the awe-inspiring mystery—the *mysterium tremendum*—that Rudolph Otto associates with the experience of the holy.

We can come to grips with the religious dimension of Eiseley's outlook at a still more basic level, however, by considering a comment Paul Tillich attributes to an unnamed philosopher. "Religion," he writes, "is what a man does with his solitariness." Solitariness, especially when painfully experienced as loneliness, is basic to Eiseley's presentation of himself, and is connected with his avoidance of the issues raised by Heard's second question: "*What am I*? How am I related to other men?" Although some mention of the latter has already been made, we now need to consider this aspect of the essays in more detail so that we can better understand the applicability of Tillich's statement to Eiseley.

In one memorable passage he refers to a certain South African skull, housed in a metropolitan museum, about which he says, "I have never looked longer into any human face than I have upon the features of that skull" (*IJ*, 127–28). Since anyone reading extensively in Eiseley's work might easily begin to long for the warmth of a human smile or the touch of a human hand, this chilling assertion is entirely credible. Sometimes it seems as though only he is left alive, that the rest of the world has become a vast graveyard. As a result his vision may make some readers recoil. Others, on the contrary, may be prompted to dismiss his outlook—in the way that some have done with Thomas Wolfe's—as being insufficiently mature. Yet, if we are going to read Eiseley, there can be no escaping involvement with his pervasive sense of isolation.

The personal sources of Eiseley's loneliness are revealed in the memories he recounts of his childhood and youth. Collected in Chapter 2, these memories suggest that he saw himself as destined to lead an isolated life. In any event such an aching and persistent sense of being alone permeates his books that it can be understood as the wellspring of his work. Nor is it just his individual isolation that concerns him. Like the orphaned Ishmael at the end of *Moby-Dick*, he reminds us that separateness is the condition of all mankind.

Of course there are times when Eiseley depicts himself as an adult in relation to people he knows. He devotes a chapter, for instance, to the year—"one of the happiest of my life" (*ASH*, 114)—that he and two other students spent as roommates in the old International House in Philadelphia. He also has only good memories to recount of Frank Speck, his mentor and later his friend at Penn. In addition he describes two or three moments of closeness with his wife. The most noteworthy of these occurs at his mother's funeral when, trying to get at something too deep to explain, he murmurs to Mabel, "You came the whole way," and she softly replies, "Yes, Lare. . . . We came the whole way" (*ASH*, 232).

But such passages come to mind largely because of their rarity. Near the end of his autobiography Eiseley acknowledges, "I have played a certain visible role in life, but that my thoughts have often been elsewhere is quite apparent" (*ASH*, 255). Where they have been is in the night country, as he calls it, that region of the spirit where the individual has experiences removed from the light of common day (even if some of them take place with the sun overhead). Indeed, as is suggested in Chapter 1, his preoccupation with this aspect of life in his essays is a major factor in the creation of his personal myth.

Moreover, were it not for his withdrawal into the wilderness within, the essays would never have come into being. As a writer Eiseley was well aware of the positive value of loneliness. It is a necessary ingredient of the creative process, the process by which the artist and the scientist as well "bring out of the dark void, like the mysterious universe itself, the unique, the strange, the unexpected" (*NC*, 204).

Yet there is another side to this coin of creativity. Opposite the need for isolation is the desire for expression, for contact with others. Jacob Landau, a contemporary artist in a different medium from Eiseley's, puts the matter this way: "Painting is an act of withdrawing from others to realize oneself, which in turn is a means for drawing closer to others so that they may be helped to realize themselves. 'Innering' myself is both a commitment to the abyss, to loneliness, and a passionate longing for understanding and acceptance, for 'outering.' " Eiseley was also familiar with this longing, for he knew that loneliness frequently leads to such heightened self-awareness that the mind is unable to contain it. "The spirit literally cannot remain within itself," he writes. "It will talk if it talks on paper only to itself, as did Thoreau" (*NC*, 216–17).

This observation arises directly from Eiseley's own experience. Suffering once from a siege of temporary deafness that cut him off from normal communication with others, he turned for relief to the creation of a prose world out of the ghost world he felt himself to be inhabiting. Although he claims to have written only to entertain himself in the winter-long silence, his frequent use of direct address makes us aware of his need for "outering."

This stylistic habit, evident throughout his work, is most pervasive in *All the Strange Hours*. "Make no mistake," he tells the reader on the opening page, and on the closing one he repeats the same imperative. In between his writing is peppered with countless examples of the expressed or implied second-person pronoun, ranging from such incidental phrases as "you know" and "you see," to more insistent passages of direct address. In one place, for example, he interrupts a discussion of his outlook on life to say with studied nonchalance, "Perhaps you do not care for these things, my friends, but I care and I have come a weary distance. My anatomy lies bare. Read if you wish, or pass on" (*ASH*, 225). On another page, where he depicts himself thinking of his relationship with his mother while standing by her grave, he sounds more desperate as he insists, "And it was all nothing. Nothing, do you understand?" (*ASH*, 25). Passages of this sort underscore the extent of Eiseley's loneliness by calling attention to the depth of his need to reach out from the printed page, to touch the unseen reader through his words.

Nevertheless it is the content of the essays that most directly reveals his isolation. Almost all his significant experiences beyond childhood, we discover, are presented as having occurred with strangers. In this, whether consciously or not, Eiseley again reminds us of Wordsworth, and especially of his meeting on a lonely moor with the leech-gatherer. Claiming, outside the context of "Resolution and Independence," to have discovered the old man not far from his cottage in Grasmere, Wordsworth describes him within the poem as being "Like one I had met with in a dream; / Or like a man from some far region sent, / To give me human strength, by apt admonishment." The situation is similar with Eiseley. Feeling disconnected from the daylight world of ordinary social relationships, he tells of various "numinous encounters" with unusual individuals who bring him messages from the night country.

One of these takes place in the darkness of a city dump, lit only by the fires of burning rubbish. There, after stepping down from a stalled train on which he had been traveling at night, Eiseley speaks with one of the grimy attendants who holds up part of an old radio cabinet on his pitchfork. This infernal scene, with its lurid flames and dangling wires, later reminds Eiseley of an airplane crash and of a scorched skullcap he had once fit over a dead man's brains. He sees a similarity between the broken radio and the mangled skull vault, both of which bring to mind a sense of disconnection, waste, and loss. "[N]ow where are the voices and the music?" he rhetorically asks (*UU*, 28).

The darkness of a more disturbing meeting is entirely metaphoric, because it takes place on a sun-drenched prairie. Having wandered far out on a day in which it felt good to be alive, Eiseley encountered only one other human being. The man was an entomologist who gleefully carried in a bottle a new and unnamed parasite. Kept alive in the juices drained from a rabbit's belly, the "enormous glistening worm" alternately expanded and contracted, "searching blindly for the living flesh from which it had been torn" (*UU*, 134–35). What to make of this abhorrent presence in the heart of nature? Eiseley writes, "It was as though the pulse of the universe had been transferred to that obscene, monstrous body that was swelling as though to engulf the world. The more I looked, the more it appeared to grow. The high clean air of that lonely upland only made the event more unnatural, the collector's professional joy more maniacal" (*UU*, 135).

The two episodes, experienced by another, could easily have been forgotten. But they stand out in Eiseley's writing because he is one of those "capable of discerning in the flow of ordinary events the point at which the mundane world gives way to quite another dimension" (*IJ*, 164). Consequently he often feels that he has been singled out for the reception of some unusal message or revelation. In a concluding comment about the figure on the prairie, for instance, he says, "I do not comprehend to this day what it was that ordained our meeting" (*UU*, 135). This statement clearly shows that Eiseley views his experience in an uncommon way, and solitariness is an essential ingredient of it. As he says in a different context, "[A] man by himself is bound to undergo certain experiences falling into the class of which I speak" (*IJ*, 164).

Another of them, the most gothic of Eiseley's encounters, occurred "in a rural and obscure corner of the United States" (*NC*, 146). Having lost his way at evening and being overtaken by a sudden storm, he stepped forward to hail the driver of a haywagon that rumbled toward him across a plank bridge in the lowering dark. Then, for an instant, a bolt of lightning illuminated the scene, which Eiseley describes in this way:

> In that brief, momentary glimpse within the heart of the lightning, haloed, in fact, by its wet shine, I had seen a human face of so incredible a nature as still to amaze and mystify me as to its origin. It was—by some fantastic and biological exaggeration—two faces welded vertically together along the midline, like the riveted iron toys of my childhood. One side was lumpish with swollen and malign excrescences; the other shone in the blue light, pale, ethereal, and remote—a face marked by

> suffering, yet serene and alien to that visage with which it shared this dreadful mortal frame (*NC*, 147).

The significance of the Hawthornian scene was not evident to Eiseley in his youth. Yet he remembered the episode across the decades, and later became convinced that he had been granted a vision of "the double face of mankind," of all of us "galloping through a torrential landscape, diseased and fungoid, with that pale half-visage of nobility and despair dwarfed but serene upon a twofold countenance" (*NC*, 148).

It is apparent that all three of these meetings with strangers have an ontological dimension. Each one points toward an aspect of the human condition in general while being experienced concretely by Eiseley as an individual. In this sense they may all be considered as part of the quest for meaning that motivates the autobiographer and is a given of the religious man's temperament.

Eiseley's ontological concern is especially evident in two other encounters in which strangers speak oracular words. One utterance came from a derelict on a train traveling between New York and Philadelphia. When the conductor entered the car demanding tickets, the wasted figure with a dead man's eyes produced a roll of bills from his pocket and croaked, "Give me a ticket to wherever it is." Although the other passengers returned to their newspapers after the brief disturbance, Eiseley was stunned. "In a single poignant expression," he writes, "this shabby creature on a midnight express train had personalized the terror of an open-ended universe" (*NC*, 63). The other experience took place on the Wildcat escarpment in western Nebraska. During his fossil-hunting days Eiseley met a young woman there whom he calls "the last Neanderthal" because the bone structure of her face looked so primitive. With her cavernous eye sockets accentuated by the firelight so that he could see only darkness within, she stood before him one evening and asked, "Do you have a home?" The girl's question was simple and straightforward in intention, but Eiseley's meditation upon it reveals how, under the night sky, he learned of "the utter homelessness of man" (*UU*, 226–27).

Although the feeling of loneliness, cosmic in scope, comes across most explicitly in this last encounter, it is implied in all of them. For one thing Eiseley consistently presents himself as being alone at the time of his unexpected meetings. While he may not be literally by himself on every occasion, he nevertheless remains psychologically isolated. This is illustrated by the incident on the train, in which none of the other passengers seems in the least perturbed by the derelict's startling words. Second, not one of the strangers in the meetings discussed here brings any comfort or even a sense of human connection to Eiseley. On the contrary, he derives a heightened feeling of loss, terror, or alienation from each of them. It is for this very reason, in fact, that he seems destined to have crossed paths with such mysterious and evanescent figures.

Eiseley has one encounter, however, that is different from all the others, one that needs to be considered in more detail. It is with a man he calls the star thrower, and is described in a memorable essay of the same name. In the pages devoted to this meeting Eiseley presents himself, at the outset, as having been reduced to a pitiless eye in a desiccated skull. Meaning had ceased for him on the sands of Costabel and he was in a state of despair. As he puts it, "I was the inhumanly stripped skeleton without voice, without hope, wandering alone upon the shores of the world. I was devoid of pity, because pity implies hope" (*UU*, 68).

Arising shortly before dawn, he finds that "death walks hugely and in many forms" along the tidal zone of the beach (*UU*, 69). A hermit crab, for instance, is tossed up by the waves only to be devoured by waiting gulls, and the rising sun (as he knows) will quickly shrivel the mucilaginous bodies of other unprotected sea creatures. In addition, all along the shore are collectors, human beings stooping in the sand to stuff into bags various shellfish that before long will be boiled in kettles provided by the resort hotels.

Then, with the sun pressing up toward the horizon behind him, he sees in the distance a gigantic rainbow and toward its foot a lone figure who kneels down and flings an object out beyond the surf. Upon reaching the spot, he discovers that the man is searching for starfish that he picks up from tidepools and throws back out to sea.

The man speaks gently in response to a question from Eiseley, saying he collects only on behalf of the living. Eiseley in turn says that he long ago gave up collecting of any sort, whether of the living or the dead. "Death is the only successful collector," he adds tersely, before walking on with "the cold world-shriveling eye" revolving in his skull (*UU*, 72).

After this initial meeting Eiseley returns to his dark room. Two sections of the essay then follow, in which he reflects upon the nature of reality, including considerations of his personal past and the evolutionary past of the planet. As a result of these ruminations his merciless intellectual understanding is superseded by a vision of a great rift in nature, one he *feels* because he cannot deny that he loves the world. In fact, he acknowledges, it is not so much a rift as a joining: "the expression of love projected beyond the species boundary by a creature born of Darwinian struggle" (*UU*, 87). Once he comes to this realization the beam in his mind stops revolving, and he purposefully sets out again in search of the star thrower.

Finding him on a point of land that seemed to project into some domain beyond them, Eiseley says, "I understand. . . . Call me another thrower" (*UU*, 89). He then moves on down the beach, looking for starfish himself and flinging the ones that are still alive out to sea. Of this activity he writes:

> I could feel the movement in my body. It was like a sowing—the sowing of life on an infinitely gigantic scale. . . . I flung again and again while all about us roared the insatiable waters of death. . . . Somewhere far off, across bottomless abysses, I felt as though another world was flung more joyfully. I could have thrown in a frenzy of joy, but I set my shoulder and cast, as the thrower in the rainbow cast, slowly, deliberately, and well. The task was not to be assumed lightly, for it was men as well as starfish that we sought to save. . . . We had lost our way, I thought, but we had kept, some of us, the memory of the perfect circle of compassion from life to death and back again to life—the completion of the rainbow of existence (*UU*, 90).

Certainly by the end of the essay, if not before, we realize that we have been reading the account of a religious experience. Costabel, a fictitiously named coast, is a place "set apart for shipwreck" (*UU*, 73), where "[p]erhaps all men are at some time destined to arrive" (*UU*, 68). What we are presented with, in other words, is a region of the spirit externalized for the sake of narrative. Eiseley is describing a passage through the valley of the shadow of death. Because of its barrenness, the terrain is terrifying; while there he feels forsaken and alone, entirely disconnected from the sources of life. Then he sees the star thrower standing in a rainbow, and its miraculous light eventually penetrates the dark night of his soul. As a result his hopeless, agonizing loneliness becomes transformed into a creative force. Knowing that the star thrower is still at work and that others will come after them, he decides to cast his lot with life rather than succumb to the forces of death.

These considerations reveal the inadequacy of any attempt to understand "The Star Thrower" from a naturalistic perspective, such as that advocated by one critical reviewer. He asserts that "the starfish is a murderous monster—one starfish can clean out a bed of clams or oysters in a week—and it is disconcerting to hear a scientist giving himself virtuous airs for engaging in such an irresponsible caper." But despite the biological learning incorporated into the essay, Eiseley has not written it as a scientist. Instead, by identifying with the stranger on the beach "who loved not man, but life" (*UU*, 91), he dramatizes himself within the essay as one of Eliade's religious men, for whom "the appearance of life is the central mystery of the world."

It is this mystery that he chooses to support and celebrate by taking up the star thrower's cause. And in the process of doing so, as he further admits, he experiences an atavistic surge of feeling—the feeling that somewhere there is a Thrower, a hurler of stars who, "always in desolation, but not in defeat," keeps renewing light in "the boundless pit of darkness" (*UU*, 91). Thus Eiseley connects himself not only with another human being but with a transpersonal power. Pragmatic science cannot suffice for a man in a mood of this sort. Caught up on a wave of the oceanic feeling mentioned by Romain Rolland, he reminds us of Thoreau, whom Eiseley once praised for "his recognition of the creative loneliness of the individual, the struggle of man the evolved animal to live a 'supernatural life' " (*UU*, 140). When in such a state of mind one is impervious to the skepticism engendered by unremitting rationality. Eiseley is of course familiar with this skepticism; it is what brought him to the depths of despair in Costabel in the first place. By the end of the essay, however, we come to understand why he would be convinced that Freud, by dismissing the sense of awe before the great mystery of the universe as childish and irrational, had left man "somewhat shrunken and misjudged" (*ST*, 189).

Implicit in the foregoing discussion of "The Star Thrower" are three themes that need to be given close consideration because of the way they illuminate Eiseley's sensibility. They are the impulse toward compassion, the idea of a transcendent reality, and the feeling of nostalgia. In Eiseley's writing these themes are often intertwined, but for the sake of clarity I will handle each strand separately.

In itself the natural world is merciless, and Eiseley provides an account of its elemental cruelty in "One Night's Dying." There he depicts himself walking out on a stormy night along "the bay of broken things," a beach where wood is splintered, where no shell is ever left whole, and where "the bones of seamen and sea lions are pounded equally into white and shining sand" (*NC*, 172–73). As dawn approaches he notices a broken-winged gull running before him on the beach. It had been hurled against the sea cliff by the raging February wind, and he knows it will starve if dogs do not more quickly end its life. Then he sees a wild duck with a bleeding wing resting at the edge of the surf. As he draws nearer, the duck moves instinctively seaward. It successfully dives through the first two incoming waves, but its head disappears for good beneath the rise and crash of the third one. Eiseley writes, "This is the way wild things die, without question, without knowledge of mercy in the universe, knowing only themselves and their own pathway to the end. . . . This is the chaos before man came, before sages imbued with pity walked the earth" (*NC*, 173).

Of course he knows that men too can lack mercy. It was a hunter, after all, who had shattered the wing of the duck, and people in surging urban masses strike Eiseley as being even more ruthless (because conscious) than the black, insistent, irresistible waves of the sea. Yet compassion, the ability to project ourselves into the lives of others, especially across species boundaries, is something that distinguishes human beings from all other inhabitants of the planet. Evolutionary theory cannot account for this "lonely, magnificent power of humanity" (*IJ*, 46), the very same power that invested the solitary star thrower with his absurd dignity.

The thrower's reaching out in sympathy to the starfish is emblematic of the connection people feel with other forms of life. In ancient literature this connection is exemplified by the brief reunion of Odysseus and his dog Argos after a separation of almost twenty years. Eiseley calls attention to Homer's rendering of the incident, saying, "The magic that gleams an instant between Argos and Odysseus is both the recognition of diversity and the need for affection across the illusions of form" (*UU*, 23). After he too took up the star thrower's task, we recall, Eiseley mentions that through their endeavor they strove to save men as well as fish by keeping intact "the perfect circle of compassion" (*UU*, 90). Similarly Homer's scene illustrates the empathy between man and beast, a connection that paradoxically establishes the humanity of mankind. As Eiseley puts it, "One does not meet oneself until one catches the reflection from an eye other than human" (*UU*, 24).

In the course of his own wandering Eiseley caught that reflection often, especially in the eyes of dogs and cats. There was one mongrel in particular that he says he made the mistake of befriending during his hobo days. He calls it a mistake because he knew from the start that he would have to leave it behind once he gave up his temporary shelter in an abandoned freight car and took to the rails once more. "If anyone taught me anything about love," he writes, "it was that dog. It is almost fifty years since I last saw him running desperately beside the freight to which I clung. . . . I will never forget that dog's eyes" (*ASH*, 62–63).

A decade later, when he was assisting in the instruction of medical students at the University of Kansas, he entered the animal house where a colleague is depicted seizing a terrier and giving it a hypodermic injection. Although Eiseley knew that the same thing would have happened that day or another even if he were not there, he could not forget the "unutterable expression" with which the dog had looked at him before the needle sank into his flesh. " 'I do not know why I am here,' it seemed to say. 'Save me. I have seen other dogs fall and be carried away. Why do you do this? Why?' " (*ASH*, 149). Back in the laboratory, after the dissection was over and the students had filed out, Eiseley says he stood by the window trying to see the last sun for that dog whose imploring eyes continued to haunt him throughout the ensuing years.

From a much later period he also remembers a cat he found outside the apartment building where he lived in a suburb of Philadelphia. He and his wife were returning from a Christmas Eve party when they heard a plaintive cry from the shrubbery near the door. Although Eiseley says he had heard many such cries in his lifetime, this one seemed unusually eloquent as it slid "up and down the scale of animal grievance" (*ASH*, 235). In response, despite his wife's reminder about the regulations forbidding pets, he walked over to the bush. At first the cat became silent and merely looked at him, but then it emerged from the darkness and rolled over on its back in the snow at Eiseley's feet. That gesture of trust could not be rebuffed. Feeling that he was "sustaining the burden of our humanity at Christmas," he then cradled the animal in his arms and took it inside (*ASH*, 236). In this overdrawn narrative Eiseley goes on to describe the problems they had in caring for the cat and in finding a home for it, but ultimately it is the message inherent in the encounter that concerns him. As he explains it, the cat and he at last "outfaced the universe" through a combination, respectively, of trust and humane response. "For a moment," he concludes, "we closed the barrier between forms, we talked together" (*ASH*, 242).

At the beginning of the chapter devoted to this extended episode Eiseley declares that his telling the tale of a cat "does not mean that I have no sentiment for my kind" (*ASH*, 234). This unexpected statement may raise questions in our minds. Does he protest too much? Where is the evidence of his sympathy for fellow human beings? Admittedly, Eiseley does not deal with people in as much detail as he does with animals, both living and dead, but he has written some passages in which the depth of his feeling is memorably revealed.

To begin with he has a sensitive archaeologist's reverence for the past, especially as manifested in the artifact, "the humanly touched thing." Indeed, he maintains that for one who concerns himself with such matters, "the plaintive murmur of dead men and women may take precedence at times over the living voice" (*NC*, 81). Moreover, if life is to be borne with compassion, we all need to feel this sense of the past to some degree, because "nothing is more brutally savage than the man who is not aware he is a shadow" (*NC*, 85).

Two examples will serve to illustrate Eiseley's response to human beings who dwelled upon the earth before him. The first, like his reaction to the dog in the animal house, reveals a conflict between his scientific training and his more deeply rooted feelings. It is presented as a recollection from his youthful bone-hunting days. At the time he was a member of a scouting party in Texas that had unearthed a wooden frame containing the skeleton of a child wrapped in a rabbit-skin blanket along with some implements intended for its use in the afterlife. The expedition leader, in pursuit of ice-age man, was not interested in these remains because they were too recent. Nevertheless he decided to give them to "the locals" for a museum they had proposed. Eiseley knew that eventually others would be bound to discover the infant's resting place anyway, but still he felt that the cradle ought to be left undisturbed in the cavern. Archaeologist though he was, he believed that the dead should be left inviolate. The wishes of the practical leader of course prevailed, and Eiseley, who had been holding the cradle in his arms, was obliged to set it down beyond the debris of the excavation. How reluctant he was to do so is revealed in this concluding remark: "I could have spent a day up there on the great range just listening to the wind and talking to the child, murmuring to it across the centuries" (*ASH*, 99).

The other example concerns a nineteenth-century photograph of a waif asleep on a park bench in London. Eiseley's description of the girl and his response to her is best conveyed in his own words:

> She was obviously poor, her shoes were scuffed, her young body ill at ease in its graceless Victorian garments. There was despair and beauty in her face—so much beauty that it was like looking through a little window in time and wanting to reach out and touch her shoulder in compassion. I realized with difficulty that I was glancing for one unrelieved instant upon a drama and a human soul upon whom I would never look again. Where she went upon the evening of that day a century ago or what darkness swallowed her up, it would never be mine to know (*NC*, 84–85).

In part Eiseley is expressing sympathy here for the girl's forlorn condition, but her beauty—preserved in the photograph yet doomed to destruction in her actual life—adds another aspect to the passage. As in the case of the buried child, what Eiseley is principally reacting to is the pathos of mortality. His words leave no doubt that he has been hurt by the human past and does indeed have sentiment for his kind.

At the same time it is true that the expression of love in the more ordinary sense of affection for another living human being did not come easily to Eiseley. His own awareness of this is acknowledged in a poem called "A Hider's World." In his meditative fashion he begins by talking about the camouflage device of the bittern, which, when it straightens its body and points its bill upward, can resemble one of the reeds that constitute its habitat. Then he asks, "[W]hat was the / purpose / engendered / in me? To love, and conceal it all of my life / like the bittern / trying to be a reed?" (*AKA*, 46). The question apparently requires an affirmative answer, but there are nevertheless passages in Eiseley's writing that are extraordinary in their manifestation of his capacity for love.

One of the most unusual of these, as we might by now expect, concerns an experience with a complete stranger. Eiseley says that on this occasion he was sitting alone, tired and depressed, in a foreign airport. The hour was late and he had almost a whole night's wait ahead of him. Prevented from sleeping by his insomnia, he caught sight of a man at the far end of a deserted corridor limping painfully toward him with the help of a cane. At first he avoided looking at the man, but as he felt him moving closer, Eiseley's eyes were drawn back to the cripple.

It was then that he had "one of those white moments of penetration which are so dreadful," a moment wherein, with an anatomist's eye, he saw "this amazing configuration of sticks and broken, misshapen pulleys which make up the body of a man." And seeing in this way, as the man limped relentlessly on, he was prompted to entreat, "How, oh God, . . . did we become trapped within this substance out of which we stare so hopelessly upon our own eventual dissolution? How for a single minute could we dream or imagine that thought would save us, children deliver us, from the body of this death?" (*NC*, 177).

Breathing heavily, shuffling grotesquely with his heavy cane, the man was almost upon Eiseley, who did not draw back despite the odor that emanated from him. And then we are told:

> [A] strange thing happened, which I do not mean physically and cannot explain. The man entered me. From that moment I saw him no more. For a moment I was contorted within his shape, and then out of his body—our bodies, rather—there arose some inexplicable sweetness of union, some understanding between spirit and body which I had never before experienced. Was it I, the joints and pulleys only, who desired this peace so much? (*NC*, 177–78).

Did the cripple really exist? Was Eiseley actually sitting in the airport? We are left in doubt not only because of his mysterious manner of presentation, but also because he connects the entire episode to another occasion that he describes by way of introduction.

On a night that he calls "mystical," he was sitting in shadows among old books when he saw a firefly move from volume to volume, illuminating each as it went. Choosing the last book it had singled out, he immediately came upon the famous words, "Beareth all things, believeth all things, hopeth all things, endureth all things" (*NC*, 176). And these are the very words, part of St. Paul's tribute to charity, that Eiseley says came to his lips when he gathered his luggage and walked toward his plane after the experience in the airport. The encounter with the cripple thus becomes a parable of compassion, and of the peace that perfect love can bring. The projection of oneself into another (or vice versa) is something yearned for by the individual who, in his loneliness, feels himself to be disjointed or misshapen. Therefore it finally does not matter whether the episode took place in the external world, in a dream, or in Eiseley's waking imagination. The relevant point is that only a deeply compassionate man could have written it.

By now we can see, especially with the help of the biblical allusion, that there is something uncommon about the nature of Eiseley's feeling for others, something that lifts it into the realm of the religious. Its essential aspect is a lack of particularity. He does not present us with his love for some other human being who might respond in kind. Instead what we get, through specific examples to be sure, is a generalized compassion for all creatures, whether human or not, whether living or dead.

A dramatic illustration of this is provided by his account of an accident he once had. Walking to his office one afternoon, he tripped and fell face down upon the sidewalk, injuring his nose and gashing his forehead in the process. When he became aware of the widening pool of his blood on the concrete, he had a strange reaction, one so unusual that he takes the precaution of assuring us he was quite sane, albeit in a peculiarly detached way. Instead of being primarily concerned with his own wounds, as we might expect, and instead of addressing any of the people who had run to his assistance, he found himself talking directly to his blood cells. "Oh, don't go," he said. "I'm sorry, I've done for you" (*UU*, 177). What he had in mind were the phagocytes and platelets, all the microscopic living things that had been part of him and that through his carelessness were now "dying like beached fish on the hot pavement" (*UU*, 178). For the first time in his life he thought of these creatures not as odd objects under a lens but as tiny beings who lived and worked within him. "A great wave of passionate contrition, even of adoration, swept through my mind," he writes, "a sensation of love on a cosmic scale, for mark that this experience was, in its way, as vast a catastrophe as would be that of a galaxy consciously suffering through the loss of its solar systems" (*UU*, 178).

Among those passages in his essays where Eiseley might appear to be posturing in his presentation of himself, is this single sentence: "Perhaps it is always the destined role of the compassionate to be strangers among men" (*UU*, 192). Affected, we may well think. Too much of the Shelleyan sense of falling upon the thorns of life. Yet, if we pay close attention to episodes such as those previously discussed, we may revise our opinion because of acquiring a clearer idea of what he means by compassion. After all, how many people might have reacted as he did to the accident on the sidewalk? Two that come to mind are St. Francis and Albert Schweitzer. For the most part, of course, Eiseley does not belong in their company because of the extraordinary ways in which they put their compassion into practice in their lives. Yet the sensibility that emerges from his essays *is* uncommon. It can be properly understood only in the light of attitudes that we customarily associate with noteworthy religious figures.

Underlying these attitudes or ideas is Eiseley's profound sense of loneliness. "Even as we project love and affection upon others," he writes, "we endure a loneliness which is the price of all individual consciousness—the price of living" (*IP*, 48). Compassion, in other words, cannot cure loneliness, which has its mysterious source in the human personality. In some notes he made while working on *All the Strange Hours* Eiseley hammers home this conviction by declaring, "The solitude of the person in the body is the final ultimate divorcement of man from nature. One sees it peering out of death beds." It is in the solitary confinement of that "divorcement" that Eiseley yearns for contact not only with other creatures, both human and nonhuman, but also with some transcendent reality.

This raises a problem because, as Michael Novak has written, "The transcendent context of human life may be viewed as an illusion or as the really real by comparison with which all else is straw." Those who take the former view—followers of Freud and other proponents of the positivistic spirit going back at least as far as Francis Bacon—will not be very patient or sympathetic readers of Eiseley. Yet, with Plato as its most illustrious advocate, the other viewpoint has an even more ancient lineage in Western thought. Ever since Leibnitz it has gone by the name of the perennial philosophy, which in its metaphysics "recognizes a divine Reality substantial to the world of things and lives and minds." All romantics inevitably have some share in this metaphysical perspective, because they cannot rest content with the notion that what presents itself to our physical senses is all there is.

Eiseley's affinity with the idealist outlook is implied through a conversation he describes as having taken place between himself and Frank Speck. The two of them had gone for a stroll in the Philadelphia Zoo, where they saw a beautifully patterned wood duck swimming in a pond. " 'Loren,' Speck said, as they stood watching, 'tell me honestly. Do you believe unaided natural selection produced that pattern? Do you believe it has that much significance to the bird's survival?' " (*ASH*, 94).

In a long and considered response, Eiseley says he does not doubt that every creature arose from something older and more primitive, but he admits to being troubled over the way this came about:

> Sometimes it seems very clear, and I satisfy myself in modern genetic terms. Then, as perhaps with your duck, something seems to go out of focus, as though we are trying too hard, trying, it would seem, to believe the unbelievable. I honestly don't know how to answer. I just look at things and others like them and end by mystifying myself. I can't answer in any other way. I guess I'm not a very good scientist; I'm not sufficiently proud, nor confident of my powers, nor of any human powers (*ASH*, 94).

In other words, believing that the world is too complex to be reduced to human proportions through simplifying hypotheses, he has doubts about the sufficiency of established scientific doctrine. "I know we have learned a lot," he concludes, "but the scope is too vast for us. Every now and then if we look behind us, everything has changed. It isn't precisely that nature tricks us. We trick ourselves with our own ingenuity. I don't believe in simplicity" (*ASH*, 95).

At the same time he yearns for some unitary vision, some transcendent principle of order beyond the bewildering diversity of phenomenal reality. Thus he calls attention to the enormous morphological stability of the great phyla. "They all, or most of them, survived since the first fossil records," he observes. "They do not vanish. The species alter, one might say, but the *Form*, that greater animal which stretches across the millennia, survives." Finding "a curious comfort" in this discovery, he says, "It is almost as though somewhere outside, somewhere beyond the illusions, the several might be one" (*FT*, 82). As this passage shows, Eiseley is not unwilling to extend his reach past scientific facts in order to suggest a tentative Platonism of his own.

Elsewhere, in discussing the principle of organization that inheres in all living things, he goes still further. First he points out that although life does not persist without organization, organization itself cannot be called the product of life. Then he adds, "Like some dark and passing shadow within matter, it cups out the eyes' small windows or spaces the notes of a meadow lark's song in the interior of a mottled egg. That principle—I am beginning to suspect—was there before the living in the deeps of water" (*IJ*, 26). This is an enigma that defies scientific explanation. The intricate organization of all life forms, like the crystaline pattern of a snowflake, "is an apparition from that mysterious shadow world beyond nature" (*IJ*, 27). Beyond nature? What does this mean? The phrase reminds us that we are not listening here to the voice of a scientist. Instead we are in the presence of a religious man, one who uses words in the manner of a poet to hint at a dimension of reality that cannot be brought within the purview of the laboratory.

It is a paradox of human perception that this dimension, which is traditionally spoken of as if it were above and beyond us, is often experienced as being deeply within us. St. Augustine clearly identifies this paradox in his reference to God as "deeper than the deepest recesses of my heart, and . . . higher than the highest I could reach." The most high and the most deep are really one.

What is at issue here is "the realm of the invisible." In trying to talk about it a problem inevitably arises because we find it hard to avoid words that suggest physical location in space. Eiseley himself is aware of the difficulty and quotes the anonymous medieval author of *The Cloud of Unknowing* to illustrate the point: "Be wary that thou conceive not bodily that which is ghostly, although it be spoken bodily in bodily words as be these, up or down, in or out, behind or before" (*NC*, 74). Because the conditions of modernity have sapped our traditional religious vocabulary of its vitality, we tend to shy away from words that suggest a region above and beyond us. Instead, under the influence of twentieth-century discoveries in psychology, we feel more comfortable with the notion of depth. Yet we must be careful not to conceive of the term "bodily." As long as we take this precaution we can meaningfully refer, in the words of Janet Varner Gunn, to "the depth level of lived experience," to that dimension of reality that, "though inaccessible to empirical observation, nonetheless upholds and gives meaning to the 'visible, tangible [and] palpable.' "

This level of experience has been likened by Ira Progoff to an underground stream that flows below the well of each individual self. It is the same place that the author of *The Cloud of Unknowing* had in mind when he referred to "the ground of naked being," the place where (as Progoff puts it) "we can experience unitary connection with life." No one has permanent access to this region of the spirit; temporary contact is the most that can be achieved. In addition it is no easy matter, even if one has experienced it, to articulate a sense of participation in the unity of being. But Eiseley composed one essay—"The Flow of the River"—in which he was uncommonly successful in this endeavor.

In introducing it he writes, "Once in a lifetime, perhaps, one escapes the actual confines of the flesh. Once in a lifetime, if one is lucky, one so merges with sunlight and air and running water that whole eons, the eons that mountains and deserts know, might pass in a single afternoon without discomfort" (*IJ*, 16). His depiction of how it happened with him then follows. Having walked for miles one day in the hot sun of the high plains, he came upon the Platte River. After shedding his clothes and cooling off for a while in a hole among some reeds, he felt a longing to lie back in the shallow water and gently float with the stream. What transpired when he acted upon this impulse must be conveyed in Eiseley's own words.

Picturing him with arms outstretched and face to the sun, we read:

> The sky wheeled over me. For an instant, as I bobbed into the main channel, I had the sensation of sliding down the vast tilted face of the

> continent. It was then that I felt the cold needles of the alpine springs at my fingertips, and the warmth of the Gulf pulling me southward. Moving with me, leaving its taste upon my mouth and spouting under me in dancing springs of sand, was the immense body of the continent itself, flowing like the river was flowing, grain by grain, mountain by mountain, down to the sea. I was streaming over ancient sea beds thrust aloft where giant reptiles once sported; I was wearing down the face of time and trundling cloud-wreathed ranges into oblivion. . . . I was streaming alive through the hot and working ferment of the sun, or oozing secretively through shady thickets. I *was* water and the unspeakable alchemies that gestate and take shape in water, the slimy jellies that under the enormous magnification of the sun writhe and whip upward as great barbeled fish mouths, or sink indistinctly back into the murk out of which they arose. Turtle and fish and the pinpoint chirpings of individual frogs are all watery projections, concentrations—as man himself is a concentration—of that indescribable liquid brew which is compounded in varying proportions of salt and sun and time (*IJ*, 19–20).

Eiseley's contact with the acutal river enabled him, in this instance, to get in touch with the metaphoric underground stream. In his nakedness, feeling an enormous extension of himself both in time and space, he seemed to become water itself. Being the mother element from which we all emerged, water is essential to life in scientific terms and is an ancient symbol of life in religiopoetic terms. Eiseley here combines both understandings by blending scientific knowledge with poetic prose, and in the process evokes a sense of having temporarily achieved a unitary connection with the mystery we call life.

It is mysterious, first of all, because its chemical ingredients are known but the vital spark remains secret and inscrutable. As Eiseley writes elsewhere, "[T]he minute I start breaking this strange body down into its constituents, it is dead. It does not know me. Carbon does not speak, calcium does not remember, iron does not weep" (*NC*, 51). In the second place life is mysterious because of its infinite number of appearances both at any given time and across the ages. This is the mystery that Eiseley seems to have penetrated in the river-floating episode. By experiencing an altered state of perception, an out-of-the-body consciousness, he became one with the vital element that animates (or has animated) all creatures from a brontosaurus to a frog to himself.

Later in the essay Eiseley writes about cutting a catfish out of a frozen backwater of the same river one subsequent winter. After the block of ice melted in the bucket where he put it, he discovered to his surprise that the fish was still alive. Throughout the winter he kept it in a tank in his house, but one spring night it jumped out and he found it dead on the floor the next morning. At the end of the anecdote Eiseley laments the loss of the fish, saying, "He had for me the kind of lost archaic glory that comes from the water brotherhood. We were both projections out of that timeless ferment and locked as well in some greater unity that lay incalculably beyond us" (*IJ*, 24). For the man who had floated with the river, there can be no doubt about this. For him, despite the concrete existence of an infinite number of living things, the transcendent is the really real.

If not loneliness, then certainly solitariness is a precondition for an awareness of this sort. It is impossible to imagine Eiseley having the river experience he describes if he had come upon the Platte in the company of others, all of whom sought to refresh themselves by splashing in the water. People in groups are necessarily concerned above all with relationships among themselves. Only the lone individual is likely to become conscious of a dimension of reality beyond the daylight world of social custom. As Eiseley makes clear in other passages, the night country has its terrors, but they are the price that must be paid for insight. It is only there that he could come to the essentially religious conviction that man "is at heart a listener and a searcher for some transcendent realm beyond himself"; and only from the perspective acquired there could he assert that beyond our human perceptions "lies the great darkness of the ultimate Dreamer" (*UU*, 55).

This last statement is reminiscent of one we have read before. In "The Star Thrower" Eiseley speaks of the sowing motion of his body as again and again he cast the starfish out to sea, and of how that motion gave rise to "a great atavistic surge of feeling," which prompted him to think that perhaps somewhere "the Thrower"—the hurler of stars in the heavens—smiled in recognition of his work

(*UU*, 91). The word that needs to be stressed here is *atavistic*, because through its use Eiseley acknowledges the presence within him of a mode of apprehension much more primitive than that adhered to by modern science. The mere existence of this primitive streak may not be peculiar to Eiseley, but his expression of primeval longings, permeated always by a feeling of nostalgia, is often uniquely memorable.

We have already confronted a specific example of Eiseley's nostalgia in "The Mist on the Mountain." There he conjures up an idyllic vision of his childhood and expresses the desire never to have left it for the world of adulthood. In another work he depicts a version of the Golden Age, an idealized time of communal endeavor and festivity, that his fancy tells him once existed in pioneer America. That epoch has been banished, he maintains, by our technological culture, which has "released urban and even rural man from the quiet before his hearth log [and] has debauched his taste" (*NC*, 141–142).

More significantly and characteristically, however, Eiseley's desire is directed toward something larger than a simpler period of personal or social history. These commonplace manifestations of nostalgia are overshadowed in his pages by a longing that embraces the past of the entire planet. He calls it a "backward yearning," and likens himself in this regard to mammals who have returned from the land to the sea, to fish who have taken to sleeping in the mud, and to birds who no longer fly (*NC*, 26). Through these comparisons he suggests that he too is a creature who longs to return to some former state of evolutionary development. "My eye," he confesses elsewhere, "is round, open, and undomesticated as an owl's in a primeval forest—a world that for me has never truly departed" (*ASH*, 144).

Although the world of the primeval forest may still reside somewhere in Eiseley's imagination, he knows that the time and place of beginnings are gone for good from the earth. His youthful meeting with the "Neanderthal" girl prompted him to realize that he would never find his true home because it lay back "down that hundred-thousand-year road on which travel was impossible" (*UU*,

226). And when it was time for him to leave the camp by the fossil quarry in the autumn, he was overcome by a strange feeling. As he puts it, "[S]omething never intended had arisen in me there by the darkening water—some agonizing, lifelong nostalgia, both personal and, in another sense, transcending the personal" (*UU*, 225).

In his study of the nature of religion Mircea Eliade makes some comments that contribute to an understanding of Eiseley here. Focusing on the beliefs and ritual practices of primitive peoples, Eliade refers to "a desire to reintegrate a primordial situation—that in which the gods and mythical ancestors were *present*." Then he adds:

> This primordial situation is not historical, it is not calculable chronologically; what is involved is a mythical anteriority, the time of origin, what took place "in the beginning," *in principio*.
>
> Now, what took place "in the beginning" was this: the divine or semidivine beings were active on earth. Hence the nostalgia for origins is equivalent to a *religious* nostalgia. Man desires to recover the active presence of the gods; he also desires to live in the world as it came from the Creator's hands, fresh, pure, and strong.

As a modern man Eiseley no longer believes in the ancient gods, and advances in geology have made the time of origins with which he is concerned roughly calculable. Nevertheless there are ways in which his outlook is analogous to that of Eliade's primitives.

Perhaps this is not surprising since Eiseley repeatedly indicates that he *is* a primitive. The reference above to his owl's eye suggests as much, and in other passages throughout his work his atavistic tendencies are made even clearer. One of these surfaces in conversation with a university administrator, in which he acknowledges that to him Frank Speck represented "the last of wild America." With Speck's death that wildness disappeared, and he says he has subsequently become estranged from his own department. The administrator replies that Eiseley, in kinship with Speck, has always been "[l]ike a man come in with furs to warm himself at the stove, but not to stay. That's what Frank knew, that's your secret" (*ASH*, 132). Eiseley's silence at this point implies that the other man is correct in his estimate. Earlier in the book, however, he mentions a difference between Speck and himself in that his mentor's people, the Iroquois, were too recent for him. "I belonged further back," he says, "back on the *altiplano* with the great grey beasts of the crossing" (*ASH*, 97). In another place he is still more explicit: "If there is any truth to the story that at death men return to the period they have loved best in life, I know well where I will awake. It will be somewhere on the cold, bleak uplands of the ice-age world, by the fire in the cave, and the watching eyes without" (*NC*, 26).

This Pleistocene period, the era during which *Homo sapiens* emerged, is for Eiseley the primordial time when the world was still "fresh, pure, and strong." At first man was at one with his surroundings, especially with his animal companions, as he walked "memoryless through bars of sunlight and shade in the morning of the world" (*IJ*, 125). But then something happened in the human brain, an event which Eiseley locates between the beginning of the first ice age and the second. "For the first time in four billion years," he writes, "a living creature . . . contemplated himself and heard with a sudden, unaccountable loneliness, the whisper of the wind in the night reeds" (*IJ*, 125). This initial stirring of self-consciousness marks the start of our specifically human development, when man began his long journey from the forest to the city.

It was to account for the profound change suffered during the course of that journey, Eiseley says, that the story of the Fall came into being. We have previously seen how he applies this myth to his own childhood, but here he makes use of it in a much larger context. To support his position he quotes other authorities, among them Coleridge and Emerson. The former asserted that "A Fall of some sort or other—the creation as it were of the non-absolute—is the fundamental postulate of the moral history of man" (*IP*, 61). And Emerson declared, "It is very unhappy, but too late to be helped, the discovery we have made that we exist. That discovery is called the Fall of Man" (*UU*, 47). Eiseley himself maintains that even an unbeliever must accept the notion, for man did in fact fall "from the grace of instinct into a confused and troubled cultural realm beyond nature, much as in the old theology man fell from a state of innocence into carnal knowledge" (*UU*, 136).

However we may wish to articulate it, the Fall is always understood as the ultimate source of the lack of wholeness or harmony in human life. What is the response of religious man to his awareness of this state of affairs? In Christian belief the alleviation of present ills has traditionally been longed for in the future, in a paradise to come. Eiseley, unmoved by the forms of present-day religion, instead adopts the stance of the primitive. Thus his nostalgia manifests itself as a longing for a return to the original paradise, the perfection of the primordial situation.

That longing has its source in man's loneliness, in his awareness that he inhabits an "invisible island" on which he is isolated from the rest of the natural world (*UU*, 164). Eiseley feels this very strongly and expresses a desire to find "a way back through the leafy curtain that has swung behind us" (*UU*, 165). Of course he knows that curtain can never really open again, but he nevertheless seeks moments of return through the exercise of his imagination, especially through a sympathy with animals. Although his compassion for other creatures has already been discussed, two more episodes need to be considered in regard to the theme of nostalgia.

The first concerns a few abandoned dogs that Eiseley saw in the rubble created by the demolition of some dilapidated row houses in Philadelphia. Unwilling to leave the place that had been their home, they sat or lay like wolves amid the wreckage "in a sort of momentary local return to the stone age" (*ASH*, 152). When he crossed the street to join them in the bitter weather, one brown dog in particular crept forward and ran his rough tongue across Eiseley's hand. In response Eiseley knelt down and spoke gravely to him. Then these extraordinary words appear in his narration of the episode: " 'If you would come out of your doors and your stonework,' the patient stroking tongue tried to persuade me, 'we could lie here in the dust and be safe, as it was in the beginning when you, the gods, lived close to us and we came in to you around the fire' " (*ASH*, 153). Not many people could have written a sentence like that. Through it we come to understand better the intensity of Eiseley's urge for the elemental and the extent of his dissatisfaction with modern life.

In primitive societies festivals are held that enable the participants to become the contemporaries of an event that occurred "in the beginning." By this means, as Eliade writes, an individual from a traditional culture "periodically finds his way into mythical and sacred time, re-enters the *time of origin*, the time that 'floweth not' because it does not participate in profane temporal duration, because it is composed of an *eternal present*, which is indefinitely recoverable." Contemporary culture offers no compelling ritual escapes from history. Anyone interested in returning to primordial time in our day must do so on his own in some entirely fortuitous and unrepeatable fashion. In "The Innocent Fox" Eiseley presents one memorable occasion when precisely this happened to him.

The episode took place on a beach. Having spent the night in a sheepskin crouching against the broken prow of an overturned boat, he became aware toward morning, as the fog began to lift, that he was not alone. Then he saw two projecting ears lit by the rising sun. They belonged to a fox pup, and Eiseley crept on his knees around the prow to a place beside him. In response the wide-eyed fox picked up a chicken bone from a pile of rubbish and shook it invitingly. Then Eiseley writes:

> It was not a time for human dignity. It was a time only for the careful observance of amenities written behind the stars. Gravely I arranged my forepaws while the puppy whimpered with ill-concealed excitement. I drew the breath of a fox's den into my nostrils. On impulse, I picked up clumsily a whiter bone and shook it in teeth that had not entirely forgotten their original purpose. Round and round we tumbled for one ecstatic moment (*UU*, 210).

Eiseley is aware that the event might seem unimportant to others, that there would be no use in his reporting it to a scientific association. Yet its significance for him was momentous. Through the simple act of playing with a young fox he says he "had been permitted to correct time's arrow for a space of perhaps five minutes—and that is a boon not granted to all men" (*UU*, 211). In the process he had also "seen the universe as it begins for all things" and discovered that it was "a tiny and laughing universe," one fit for a child (*UU*, 210).

All three of the themes we have been considering are evident in this episode. Compassion or love comes first, because it is an outgoing of Eiseley's spirit to the fox that prompts him to play with the animal. The play itself is an embodiment of nostalgia, of the desire to return to a prelapsarian, paradisal condition. And through the play, contact with a transcendent reality is fleetingly achieved in that, while romping with the fox and experiencing a kind of oneness with him, Eiseley feels that he has entered an eternal realm where clock time has no meaning.

The incident could undoubtedly be criticized as being indicative of a desire on Eiseley's part to escape responsibility for his historical existence. Eliade points out that a modern psychologist would be tempted to interpret the attitudes of religious man—as embodied in this episode, for example—as a manifestation of "nostalgia for a situation that is paradisal precisely because it is embryonic, insufficiently detached from nature." And Freud, had he read the passage, would surely have considered it to reflect a survival of infantile ego-feeling in the adult writer.

To call Eiseley's behavior childlike or primitive, however, is not necessarily to belittle it. As in the river-floating episode, he here considers himself to have been blessed by circumstances that permitted a temporary release from the burden of self-consciousness, which is a primary goal of those who adhere to the perennial philosophy. "Direct knowledge of the Ground [of being] cannot be had except by union," as Aldous Huxley has written, "and union can be achieved only by the annihilation of the self-regarding ego." There can be no doubt that an annihilation of this sort occurs in Eiseley's encounter with the young fox. For him it represents one of those moments of special grace mentioned by W. H. Hudson, and his account may even remind us of one of the better known New Testament sayings: "Except ye . . . become as little children, ye shall not enter into the kingdom of heaven."

No matter whether the episode is responded to favorably or unfavorably by the individual reader, the fact is that it clearly dramatizes the religious disposition that is fundamental to Eiseley's presentation of himself. On the other hand, once the magic circle of play was broken, once Eiseley and the fox went their separate ways, his knowledge of the infallible flight of time's arrow would inevitably have reasserted itself in his mind. The little laughing world, suffused in the light of morning, could not for long stay out of the dark shadow cast by the immense surrounding universe. And it is Eiseley's confrontation with this shadow, a confrontation none can avoid, that is the central concern of the final chapter.

V

An Artist of Autumn

> For man himself . . . has a doom upon him
> of perpetual vanishing.
>
> —Loren Eiseley

In *The Fall* Camus's mordant narrator refers to a "man who, having entered holy orders, gave up the frock because his cell, instead of overlooking a vast landscape as he expected, looked out on a wall." We quickly grasp the unstated idea. How could the monk achieve the goal of enlarging his soul to accommodate the divine if his vision was so closely confined? The theotropic mind often requires an analogue in the external world to help it explore the metaphorically vast inner regions where it hopes to find the immanent god.

Although there are no established orders that would have been suited to Eiseley's contemplative inclinations, there can be no doubt that he had a mind of this sort. And since the forms of religion arise in response to certain spiritual needs, it should not be surprising that the needs remain despite a loss of vitality in the forms that once satisfied them. Thus Eiseley, who comes across in his books as a man of almost monkish isolation, looks out at the world with a yearning that is perhaps even more intense than that experienced by solitary seekers in less anxious centuries. For he is a representative modern man, that figure "of ruinous countenance from whom the gods have hidden themselves" (*UU*, 171).

Yet, as Eiseley well knew, the situation of modern individuals is, in evolutionary terms, merely an extension of a certain specialization that arose during the Pleistocene period. One science writer has put the matter this way:

> [M]an owes his evolutionary success almost entirely to the precocious development of his brain. As his brain became larger and more complex, his powers of reason increased, and with them the capacity for what is generally termed 'conceptual thought'. . . . This marked the beginning of an entirely new chapter in evolutionary progress. In evolving man, Nature had produced an organism with a mind that was not only ideally planned to control its flexible and well-adapted body, but was actually able to escape into the realms of abstract thought.

Eiseley treats the same phenomenon in language that is designed to help us sense its magnitiude. He observes that as a result of the unprecedented development in brain size, man "was becoming something the world had never seen before—a dream animal—living at least partially within a secret universe of his own creation" (*IJ*, 120). In other words man was crossing over from the world of nature to the world of culture. As Eiseley painfully recognizes, however, that achievement was purchased only at the cost of shattering "[t]he Eden of the eternal present that the animal world had known for ages" (*IJ*, 121).

The heavy price we must pay for self-awareness leads Eiseley to label man the "oracular animal," one who, bereft of instinct, "must search constantly for meanings" (*UU*, 144). Nowadays it is customary to distinguish three broad fields of endeavor—religion, science, and art—within which this search is conducted. As Richard Carrington points out, all three have their origin in "a common instinct of wonder" and were constituents of "a single mental process" in primitive thought. In considering Eiseley's own search as contained in his essays, we become aware of a survival (or recurrence) of this outlook.

For one thing, despite his melancholy, Eiseley never lost the sense of wonder that Rachel Carson has singled out as being of such importance in human life. Again and again in his writing he prompts us to remember—to *see*—that nature "is one vast miracle transcending the reality of night and nothingness" (*FT*, 171). It is as if he himself had come from elsewhere and were continually amazed by his surroundings on this planet. As he puts it, "For many of us the biblical bush still burns, and there is a deep mystery in the heart of a simple seed" (*FT*, 8).

Second, if we reflect upon his essays as a whole, we realize that science, religion, and art are not compartmentalized in them, that the three seem to be aspects of a single mental process. By profession he was a scientist, an anthropologist who devoted special attention to the theory of evolution. At the same time he was aware that modern science, for all the sophistication of its methods and instruments, could not get below a certain depth in its efforts to explain the physical world. The enigma of life would always elude its grasp. Even in his first book, therefore, he mentions having found the scientific method somewhat confining, and in a later essay he admits to having "abandoned certain of the logical disciplines of [his] youth" (*ST*, 219).

In place of them, as we have seen, Eiseley adopts the less austere approach of the literary naturalist. Contrary to the laboratory scientist, for whom the phenomena of the universe are objective facts that he must try to understand by discovering their underlying patterns or principles, the naturalist makes no effort to distance himself from the objects of his study. His more personal outlook suggests that "there is a natural history of *souls*, nay, even of man himself, which can be learned only from the *symbolism* inherent in the world about him" (*NC*, 48, my emphasis). The two italicized words are not part of the scientific vocabulary. By using them in this context Eiseley shows his willingness to enter the domain of religion, and even to obscure our customary distinction between religion and science.

What of his art? Since without it the essays would not exist, we must ultimately see it as the primary instrument of Eiseley's lifelong quest. It is not only the vehicle for the conveyance of his religious and scientific outlook, but it is also the means by which (in varying degrees) he lures us into participating in his vision. Eiseley, it must be admitted, is not especially noteworthy for any original insights into the problems examined by scientists and theologians. Instead it is his evocative way of treating them that is most memorable. Eiseley the author thus functions chiefly as a poet, which means that the principal effect of his writing is "not to inform the reader but to transform him."

By this route we are led back to the beginning, back to a consideration of Eiseley's brand of personal storytelling. He was very much aware of himself as an artist, of course, as is revelaed in explicit statements he makes about the sources of his work. The most extended and significant of these—the passage in which he compares a writer's mind to a painter's loft—has already been discussed in Chapter 1. Elsewhere he puts the matter more succinctly, saying, "This is the way of it, I think. One has just so many pictures in one's head which, after one has stared at them long enough, make a story or an essay" (*ASH*, 161).

In addition Eiseley calls self-conscious attention to his function as a storyteller in some of his passages of direct address. In introducing an anecdote from his school days, for instance, he writes, "Yet bear with me a moment. I would like to tell a tale, a genuine tale of childhood" (*UU*, 57). And as a lead-in to the account of his meeting with the "Neanderthal" girl he says, "Suppose that there still lived . . . but let me tell the tale, make of it what you will" (*UU*, 219). In fact, as my discussion has shown again and again, Eiseley is an irrepressible teller of tales. Even when it is not his main intention to narrate part of his life story, he freqently uses little stories purportedly taken from his own experience for purposes of illustration. His essays are rich in personal anecdotes.

Still he is more than merely a rather old-fashioned raconteur, for in at least one significant passage he suggests a good deal about his myth-making potential. Delving deep into his own sensibility he writes:

> Man, for all his daylight activities, is, at best, an evening creature. Our very addiction to the day and our compulsion, manifest through the ages, to invent and use illuminating devices, to contest with midnight, to cast off sleep as we would death, suggest that we know more of the shadows than we are willing to recognize. We have come from the dark wood of the past, and our bodies carry the scars and unhealed wounds of that transition. Our minds are haunted by night terrors that arise

> from the subterranean domain of racial and private memories (*UU*, 195).

Eiseley's private memories, arranged in my second chapter so as to form a coherent account of his childhood and youth, reveal the individual basis for our understanding of him as an Ishmael figure. The transpersonal sources of that mythic image are less easily identified, but they can be envisioned as welling up in racial (and supraracial) memories.

Eiseley's access to such nebulous material is connected with his ability to penetrate (in Shakespeare's phrase) "the dark backward and abysm of time." In part this is a result of his learning what scientists have discovered about our evolutionary past. But his scientific knowledge seems to have aroused in him a deeper, prerational apprehension. Some sense of this is conveyed in the previously discussed accounts of his descent into the Slit, and of his ride on horseback from a green mountain meadow to a desolate arroyo far below. It comes out also in sudden, startling perceptions. He tells us, for example, that he has sat listening to a great singer in a modern concert hall, and at the same time has "heard far off as if ascending out of some black stairwell the guttural whisperings and bestial coughings out of which that voice arose" (*IJ*, 93). Elsewhere he describes his disturbing vision, while standing on a lecturer's rostrum, of a great tree trunk stretching loathsomely behind him along the floor. Trembling there with book and spectacles, he realizes that he is himself "a many-visaged thing that has climbed upward out of the dark of endless leaf-falls, and has slunk, furred, through the glitter of blue glacial nights" (*FT*, 168).

In his metaphoric fashion Eiseley claims to have been "compacted out of glacial dust and winter cold" (*ASH*, 144). This is his way of reminding us of his origins in the central plains, and one way of suggesting why the Pleistocene had such a powerful hold upon him. He could not forget that man "had come with the great ice," that (in a manner of speaking) "the ice had made him" (*ST*, 237). And in his writing Eiseley succeeds in conveying the sense that his breath partakes of the breath from that dank door, that the coldness released by it mixes with the marrow in his bones, and that the darkness from behind it haunts his mind. Especially the darkness, which he also refers to as the night tide, "because that is the way you come to feel it—invisible, imperceptible almost, unless it is looked for—and yet, as you grow older you realize that it is always there, swirling like vapor just beyond the edge of the lamp at evening and similarly out to the ends of the universe" (*NC*, 32).

Although Eiseley was attracted to the darkness and even says at one point that he loved it (*NC*, 27), he admits that, like the rest of mankind, he also feared it. That fear is embodied in rats, "the real agents of the night," about whom he tells several anecdotes (*NC*, 33). It is similarly illustrated in the account of a walk he took across the plains at night, during which he had unnerving encounters with various animals. "Having journeyed once along the dark side of the planet," he writes, "I am willing to testify that it is a shifting and unmapped domain of terrors" (*NC*, 44).

But those terrors need not assume external form. They can also take shape in the mind because of our knowledge that for each of us one night will be unending. This knowledge, which distinguishes human beings from all other animal species, is in itself fearful. Primitive man tried to cope with it by means of magic, and Eiseley—like all artists—can also be seen as a magician. He has a religious sensibility and a great deal of scientific understanding, but in the essays verbal magic is his ultimate resource. In this sense he is like the primitive caster of spells, hoping through words to keep at bay the powerful forces of death and disorder that threaten to erupt from the surrounding dark.

As I have argued from the start, story in general serves this important purpose, for against a background of chaos and incomprehension the teller of tales establishes a model of order and meaningfulness. The ending of *Beowulf* provides an excellent illustration of the point. We are told that after fifty years of wise kingship following the victories of his youth, the hero is called upon to undertake one last battle. This time it is with the dragon, an ancient emissary of the dark, who has been terrorizing the region. With the help of a single retainer the aged champion succeeds in killing the monster, but he is mortally wounded in the struggle, and the epic ends with his funeral. While the ordonnance of the poem as a whole holds in suspension the violent world of the Teutonic warriors, the atmosphere of its concluding section is permeated by a sense of impending disaster. We are specifically informed, for one thing, that Beowulf's people can now expect to be destroyed by their enemies. More generally, we are prompted to believe that, just as the sky swallows the smoke from Beowulf's funeral pyre, so will the forces of darkness ultimately overwhelm all human endeavor. The ending of the story, in other words, implies the return of chaos.

Behind this conclusion may lie the belief in pagan Germanic religion that even the gods are not immortal. It is prophesied in Nordic myth that after human civilization is destroyed by a devastating ice age, Odin and the other gods of Asgard will contend one last time with the monsters and demons of chaos led by Loki. In this fierce encounter, known as Ragnarok, the irrational powers of darkness will finally prevail and the universe itself will be destroyed by fire. Although it is also prophesied that eventually a new cosmos will emerge from the ashes of the old, one in which a different generation of gods and men will live together in peace, the projected golden age carries no imaginative force in the stories of the peoples of northern Europe.

All this changed when Christianity triumphed in the West. Then Jesus, whose life story ends not with death but resurrection, became the new culture hero. Grafting itself onto the ancient Greek understanding of human existence as analogous to the cycle of the seasons, the mythic rebirth in Christian belief occurs during the annual period of renewal in the natural world.

Now, with the decline in the vitality of the Christian story, the consolation that it embodies has for many modern people been lost. While Thoreau was able to overcome this loss by constructing a rebirth ritual of his own based on the seasonal rhythms of nature, others find themselves once again facing the fearful prospect of everlasting darkness unaided. Hemingway provides a memorable literary illustration of this predicament in "A Clean, Well-Lighted Place." In that short story an old man, neatly dressed and decorous in behavior, likes to sit late into the night in a well-lit cafe. There are also two waiters in the story, the older of whom recognizes the old patron's need and his merit. Like him, the waiter does not enjoy going back to his dark room. No legendary dragon waits for him there, but the darkness is dreadful nevertheless because it signifies "a nothing that he knew too well." In the face of this darkness, this nothing, all he requires is "a certain cleanness and order." These allow both the waiter and the patron to live their lives with some sense of dignity and propriety, which is no mean achievement even if it is not heroic in the grand manner.

Like Beowulf and the two Hemingway characters, Eiseley has no hope that might serve to temper his sense of death's finality. Yet he does something unusual in confronting his awareness of that endless night. Because life for him is "a magnificent and irrecoverable good" that exists for only a short while within each of us (*ASH*, 246), he celebrates autumn, the last stronghold of life against the onslaught of wintry darkness and death. And because the importance of the autumnal theme in Eiseley's work as a whole needs to be recognized, his handling of it deserves separate consideration.

When he was in his seventieth year Eiseley worked on a collection of poems, not published until after his death, called *Another Kind of Autumn* (1977). The title would have been appropriate for any man of his age, but in Eiseley's case it was simply the last sounding of a theme that had first been struck, remarkably enough, in his very first piece of published prose. "Autumn—A Memory," a sketch of less than two pages, had appeared fifty years before in the October 1927 issue of Wimberly's *Prairie Schooner*. At the time Eiseley had just turned twenty, but he was already acutely aware of time's passing. In the sketch he meditates upon a solitary visit he presents himself as having made to an Aztec ruin during some previous autumn. Taking us back with him to the stillness of that fading afternoon, he conjures up images of the long-dead Indians who had once lived among the crumbling walls: "There were visions of the laboring copper bodies that built this place under the blazing sun. . . . There were generations, there were brave little friendships, hatred and feasts and there was love." He also wonders, with no hope of being answered, how those people all came to die—whether in battle, or because their harvests burned, or through the displeasure of some offended god. A few lines from the end, in a sentence that anticipates his mature style, all he can do is acknowledge that "I was a shadow among shadows, brooding over the fate of other shadows that I alone strove to summon up out of the all-pervading dusk."

Eiseley's preoccupation with this season is deeply rooted in his own life, for he never forgot that he was a belated son, born when his father was forty, and the offspring of an unhappy marriage. These conditions of his origin lead him to say that he was "an autumn child surrounded by falling leaves" (*ASH*, 15). The implication is that destiny was at work, that he was a man marked for endings from the very start. In any event he dwells on the autumn theme at or near the end of three of his most noteworthy books—*The Immense Journey*, *The Unexpected Universe*, and *All the Strange Hours*.

In the concluding chapter of the first of these, published when he was fifty, Eiseley imagines himself taking an autumn walk. Wearing a hat and an old jacket, he goes outdoors on a day "when the leaves are red, or fallen, and just after the birds are gone" (*IJ*, 195). After climbing over a wall, he walks across "an unkempt field full of brown stalks and emptied seed pods," then comes to a wood where he finds a place to rest and consider "the best way to search for the secret of life" (*IJ*, 195–96). Eiseley's writing here calls self-conscious attention to his stance as an old-fashioned naturalist, one motivated by loving curiosity to explore the visible world in hopes of getting closer to its invisibly beating heart. He considers the season appropriate to his purpose because hectic activity and green leaves are not around to confuse the issue. Instead, as he writes, "The underlying apparatus, the hooks, needles, stalks, wires, suction cups, thin pipes, and iridescent bladders are all exposed in a gigantic dissection" (*IJ*, 196). Because these essentials provide "an unparalleled opportunity to examine in sharp and beautiful angularity the shape of life," he determines from henceforth to give autumn his "final and undivided attention" (*IJ*, 196–97).

Unlike the youthful sketch, which is pervaded by a romantic melancholy, this vigorous passage reflects the attitude of one who is aware of growing older and wishes to conserve his outwardly directed energies. In the two other autumnal episodes, however, Eiseley's attention once again takes a more inward turn. That in itself would result in a tonal change, but in addition both of them were published when he was much closer to the end of his life.

The earlier of the two, part of the last chapter of *The Unexpected Universe*, came out when Eiseley was sixty-two. He begins the essay by pondering the "slow-burning oxidation" in the brain that enables it to hoard memories (*UU*, 213), and he is subsequently reminded of a wild-plum thicket in Nebraska that he visited one autumn during his youth. The fallen plums contained a simpler version of "the mystery hidden in our heads," he writes. "They were hoarding and dispersing energy while the inanimate universe was running down around us" (*UU*, 217–18). On the last pages of the chapter he comments again on the plum thicket, this time in connection with a second visit he made to it on an autumn walk years later. He returned partly just to see if it was still there, but also because he remained puzzled by the "strange hoarding and burning at the heart of life" (*UU*, 231).

This much is reminiscent of the passage from *The Immense Journey* in that it suggests a continuing concern with the mysteries of the organic world. But the mood changes when he makes a different connection between the plums and himself. With his head grown heavy and the smoke from the autumn fields seeming to penetrate his mind, he says he felt like dropping all his memories just as the fruit fell about him from the trees. His desire was "to strew them like the blue plums in some gesture of love toward the universe all outward on a mat of leaves. Rich, rich and not to be hoarded, only to be laid down for someone, anyone, no longer to be carried and remembered in pain" (*UU*, 232). In this frame of mind he leaned farther back into the leaves and was overcome by a strange yet soothing feeling, one he had never had before. "Perhaps

I was no longer *Homo sapiens*," he imagines. "Perhaps all I was, really, was a pile of autumn leaves seeing smoke wraiths through the haze of my own burning" (*UU*, 232). Letting go, he had the sensation, in other words, of being no longer partially separate from nature but of returning wholly to it. Although a harbinger of the terminal loss of consciousness, the experience in this context is far from frightening. Instead it is reminiscent of a familiar line from "Ode to a Nightingale," in which Keats's lyric speaker admits that many a time he has been "half in love with easeful Death."

The final passage is contained in the last of Eiseley's books to appear during his lifetime. *All the Strange Hours* was published when he was sixty-eight years old, and is the autobiography he was unable to write when younger. There he turns to an explicit consideration of the autumn theme a few chapters from the end, being concerned this time to demonstrate its applicability to his life within the context of his family background.

He begins by referring to the dreams that plague him, some of which prompt him to strike out fiercely in the dark, while others cause him to weep or pant in fear without apparent cause. He also mentions his bouts of sleeplessness, during which times the persistent coming and going of pictures in his brain is beyond his control. Then he adds,

> This is the beginning of age as all my family have known age: my grandmother Corey, who periodically cried out desperately in her sleep for help but who, upon being awakened, never confided what it was she feared; or my mother, who finally stalked the dark house sleepless at midnight; or my father, who in the great influenza epidemic of 1917–1918 came home unassisted, went to his room, and lay quietly for days without medical attention, only his intelligent eyes roving the ceiling, waiting for which way the dice would fall and not, I believe now, caring overmuch (*ASH*, 233).

He explains all these behaviors as final efforts on the part of the individuals mentioned to order the meaning of their lives. This, he observes, is "the human autumn before the snow" (*ASH*, 233).

If spring is the season of bright promise, then fall is the time of disillusionment. Hope, the expectation of some fancied fulfillment, gives way to anguished recollection and (often) the fear of death. As Eiseley puts it, "Oncoming age is to me a vast wild autumn country strewn with broken seedpods, hurrying cloud wrack, abandoned farm machinery, and circling crows. A place where things were begun on too grand a scale to complete" (*ASH*, 234). The imagery would not be the same for everyone, of course, but he believes that the essential feeling is universal. Consequently his intention in *All the Strange Hours* is "to bespeak, in some fashion, the autumn years of all men" (*ASH*, 234).

If we pause to take a long view, we can now see that the totality of Eiseley's work may be said to embody the natural history of his soul. The beginning of the story is easy to define since it adheres to an aspect of the fable mentioned by Edwin Muir, the movement from innocence to experience through the agency of the Fall. The long middle part has no clearly marked stages, but it is dominated by the Ishmael figure who wanders through the wilderness of his individual life in search of wisdom. This is a lonely undertaking in which the seeker reads nature's signs in the world outside himself, looking for meanings that have a bearing on his own interior world, the domain that somehow connects him in its depths with a transcendent realm where oneness of being is to be found. That quest is never completed, however, and as the end draws nearer Eiseley the pilgrim vacillates between apprehension and anticipation.

The apprehension is common enough, since no one can remain immune to dread when faced with extinction. Nevertheless Eiseley's treatment of it is enhanced through his planetary perspective. Because he knows that time extends millions of millennia behind us and lies incalculably far ahead of us, he offers the following advice in words that allude to one of his own poems: "Worship, then, like the Maya, the unknown zero, the procession of the time-bearing gods" (*ASH*, 249). Still he does not let his awareness of these vast reaches of time prevent him from seeing that each individual life, brief though it is, imitates the situation of the world at large. Billions of years ago it emerged from the void, and at some time in the unforseeable future it too will return to sunless oblivion. Thus the darkness that exists both before and after our separate lives is a microcosm of the macrocosmic plight of the planet. Understood in this way, the autumn of Eiseley's life mirrors in miniature the prelude to the destruction of our universe, which, according to scientific prediction, will be even more deadly that that envisioned in Nordic myth.

The anticipation of the end is a different matter. Others have surely felt it, but Eiseley's way of handling it is unmistakably his own. The experience in the plum thicket provides one illustration of this anticipatory feeling; another is contained in a still more striking acount of his visit to a great hill in Montana.

After delivering a lecture in Concord, Massachusetts, Eiseley had flown west. There, while wandering over a sunbeaten upland, he found "a quartz knife that had the look of ten thousand years about it." He says that it was "as clean as the sun," and that suddenly he realized what Thoreau had been thinking about in regard to all the arrowheads he found scattered around the countryside. "They were free at last," Eiseley declares. "They had aged out of human history, out of corruption." Following this insight he was overcome with an exceptional feeling that he explains in this way: "I too had taken on a desert varnish. I might have been a man but, if so, a man from whom centuries had been flayed away. I was being transmuted, worn down." In this mood he lay on the ground and drifted off to sleep, all the while feeling that he was stiffening into immobility, "freezing into the agate limbs of petrified trees." Nor was there anything to fear. On the contrary, he says, "I sighed a little with the cleanliness of that release. I slept under the great sky" (*ST*, 243–45).

Although we are told that this experience literally took place in July, its atmosphere is as autumnal as that of the plum-thicket episode, and it helps us to understand how Eiseley's self-identification with the season preceding winter is another way he has of mythologizing his life. Just as the mood of apprehension has connections with the prophecy of the fabled Ragnarok, so the mood of anticipation is related in an unexpected way to the mythic pattern of innocence/fall/recovery-of-innocence. In Eiseley's case neither a resurgence of spring nor the belief in a resurrection is needed to complete the pattern. Instead the wished-for fulfillment is a consequence of his backward yearning, of his nostalgic longing for a return to some primordial situation where time and self-consciousness have no meaning. In other places he projects himself into a more primitive human condition in the ice-age world; here, in the episodes set in the plum thicket and on the hill in Montana, he imagines himself merging with nonhuman and even nonorganic matter. Thus we can see that Eiseley's treatment of the autumn theme, whether handled with apprehension or with anticipation, provides still further evidence of his need to invest his individual life with significance by placing it within a cosmic context.

In one of his *Texts for Nothing* Samuel Beckett has his monologist say, "[N]o need of a story, a story is not compulsory, just a life, that's the mistake I made, one of the mistakes, to have wanted a story for myself, whereas life alone is enough." It would be possible to argue that this attitude represents an extreme form of modern heroism on the grounds that extraordinary courage is required to face life without a story. On the other hand, because of its absence of meaning, storyless living can also be seen as scarcely human. As Eiseley has written, "No longer, as with the animal, can the world be accepted as given. It has to be perceived and consciously thought about, abstracted, and considered" (*UU*, 32). To give up on this endeavor, no longer to strive to make sense out of the welter of phenomena with which we are confronted, is therefore to relinquish an essential part of our humanity. Despite his awareness that "life was never given to be bearable" (*IP*, 81), Eiseley refused to abandon his own search for meaning. As with many other autobiographical writers from St. Augustine onward, he struggled to assert his humanity by telling stories—and ultimately a Story—about himself.

One final illustration of this effort is contained in a childhood tale concerning his whittling of small wooden crosses that he then painted with liquid gilt. How he used them and what became of them is explained in these words:

> I placed them over an occasional dead bird I buried. Or, if I read of a tragic, heroic death like those of the war aces, I would put the clipping

> . . . into a little box and bury it with a gold cross to mark the spot. One day a mower in the empty lot beyond our backyard found the little cemetery and carried away all of my carefully carved crosses. I cried but I never told anyone. How could I? I had sought in my own small way to preserve the memory of what always in the end perishes: life and great deeds (*ASH*, 29).

Eiseley's original account of this episode is told to W. H. Auden, who comments that "it was a child's effort against time" (*ASH*, 29). A similar effort was made by the adult Eiseley through the writing of essays, even though the deeds preserved thereby are not great in any traditional sense. The point is that he again sought to make a mark in defiance of the scythe-wielding mower.

Because of all the anonymous monuments that have been found throughout the world, Eiseley, as an archaeologist, is well aware of the universality of mankind's desire to leave some sign of his temporary presence on the earth. He invites us especially to consider the huge heads—survivals of the lost Olmec culture—that can still be seen in the jungles of eastern Mexico. They typify for him the work of groups of artisans from all over the globe, each of which arose to place "its stamp, the order of its style, upon surrounding objects, only to lapse again into the night of time" (*IP*, 91). Most readers are doubtless more accustomed to think of this same drive as it is manifested in the artworks of particular individuals. Each of Michaelangelo's sculptures and paintings, for instance, constitutes a "mark" that has enabled its creator to overcome in a way the destructiveness of the reaper. The autobiographical artist is similarly motivated, but the material he has to work with is his own life and character. In a sense, then, the task that occupies him is the creation—or, perhaps more accurately, the re-creation—of himself.

The world's best life-writers, as I have maintained from the beginning, have all accomplished this task in memorable fashion. Montaigne is a landmark case in point from the European past, while Henry Thoreau and Henry Adams are famous American examples. Eiseley's achievement is admittedly not on their level. On the one hand, his pieces are too dispersed to compare favorably with the concentrated effect created by the authors of *Walden* and *The*

Education of Henry Adams. On the other hand, Eiseley's work does not have the variety of the *Essays*, which means that his adventures of the self are more limited than Montaigne's.

Like them, nevertheless, he was motivated by what Alfred Kazin calls the desire "to make a home for oneself, on paper, despite Milton's *blind Fury with the abhorréd shears, who slits the thin-spun life*." In attempting to fulfill that desire, Eiseley, like his predecessors, inevitably created a myth of his own life. As C. G. Jung unequivocally declared, "What we are to our inward vision, and what man appears to be *sub specie aeternitatis*, can only be expressed by way of myth." And of his individual endeavor in *Memories, Dreams, Reflections* he added, "Whether or not the stories are 'true' is not the problem. The only question is whether what I tell is *my* fable, *my* truth."

Throughout this book my goal has been to elucidate Eiseley's fable, Eiseley's truth. In the course of doing so I gained some insight into how closely his work as a writer obliged him to consider the issue of personal identity. With characteristic obliqueness he acknowledges his own awareness of this confrontation on one of the pages of *All the Strange Hours*. There he pictures his father coiling his fist and making him shiver as he read,

> He was a kinde of Nothinge
> Until he forged himself a name (*ASH*, 183).

Clyde Eiseley may actually have spoken these words from Shakespeare, but if so he would have declaimed the entire passage:

> He was a kind of nothing, titleless,
> Till he had forged himself a name o' the fire
> Of burning Rome (*Coriolanus*, V, i, 13–15).

In their original context the words are critical of Coriolanus, who, after attaining the height of power, refused to recognize his former friends. Eiseley's purposeful abridgement of the lines, however, gives them a positive turn and emphasizes their application to himself as an artist.

This concern with his name is also suggested by the elimination of his middle initial at the time *The Immense Journey* came out. Everything he had published earlier bore his conventional name, Loren C. Eiseley; thereafter, none of his books included the "C" on the title page. After calling attention to this fact, Professor Carlisle rightly comments that since names are intrinsically bound up with the notion of identity, the changing of one's name either "announces . . . an intention to be different" or "recognizes that one already is so." No one would question that Walter Whitman's dropping of two letters from his first name signaled a profound change in his life. By the same token Eiseley's elimination of one letter seems to reflect his realization that, at almost fifty years of age, he had finally found his true voice, which (as with all autobiographical writers) communicates his sense of identity on the printed page.

That voice, as I have endeavored to show, is given added resonance by Eiseley's presentation of himself as a modern Ishmael. In turn this mythic identification helped him overcome the feeling, developed during childhood and youth, of being a kind of nothing. It was through his personal essays, from the time of *The Immense Journey* onward, that he succeeded in forging himself a name, and it is this Loren Eiseley with whom we have been concerned throughout. Telling stories in quest of his personal truth, becoming the product of his own artifice, he not only dominates the pages of his essays but also assumes a magnified stature in our minds after we have put his books down. He is the man we remember.

NOTES

The numerals to the left below refer to the pages of my text on which the relevant passages appear. Each passage is identified by a few key words, usually simply the ones with which it begins. I have used shortened titles here, but all my sources are fully identified in the bibliography.

I Approaching Eiseley's Essays

1. "a golden era of nonfiction": Zinsser, *Writing Well*, p. 56.
"The modern American essay": *Best American Essays, 1986*, p. ix.
"restored the essay's place": *Best American Essays, 1988*, p. xv.
2. "[t]he public and the private": Holmes, *Footsteps*, p. 175.
3. "At a very early period": Chopin, *The Awakening*, p. 57.
5. "I feel a little wistful": This letter and the Guggenheim application mentioned in the next sentence are among the extensive Loren Corey Eiseley Papers (UPT 50 E36) housed in the University of Pennsylvania Archives. The letter is in Box 9, File VI, and the portion of the application I refer to is in Box 25, File X.
As James M. Schwartz: Schwartz, "Loren Eiseley," p. 856.
"tend to project the world": Kazin, "Self as History," p. 75.
6. "The supreme expression": van der Post, *Patterns*, p. 3.
8. "Order is an internal stability": Forster, *Two Cheers*, p. 90.
"How can man": Forster, p. 91.
10. "the editor of his own life": Zinsser, "Writing and Remembering," p. 24.
"So when you're writing": Baker, "Life with Mother," p. 49.
"*the monolithic impact*": Pascal, *Design and Truth*, p.188.
11. Adams said that he used: All quotations from Adams in this and the succeeding paragraph are from *The Education*. They can be found (in the order they appear in my text) on pp. 512, 511, and 472.

Consequently a pattern is established: For help in discerning this pattern I am indebted to George Hochfield, *Henry Adams*, pp. 120–21.

13. "the individual seen": Gusdorf, "Conditions and Limits," p. 45.
    He acknowledges the difficulty: Thoreau, *Walden*, p. 258.
    "For a biographer": Edel, "Mystery of Walden Pond," p. 65.
    "I am now going upstairs": Baker, "Life with Mother," p. 47.
14. "continuing autobiography": Interview with H. H. Broun.
    Autobiography in this mode: Spengemann, *Forms of Autobiography*, p. 73. The words quoted in the next sentence in my text appear on the same page.
15. "a chronicle bedevilled": Cooke, "Hero in Autobiography," p. 587.
    "shun the foregone conclusions": Spengemann, p. 73.
    "It's as if": Conversation in Lincoln with Gaffney, July 10, 1981.
    Eiseley himself alluded: Interview with Broun.
16. "both a citizen and a pilgrim": Auden, *Dyer's Hand*, p. 279.
    The actual event: Christianson, *Fox*, pp. 110–11.
18. "haunted by the failure": Christianson, p. 104.
19. "to make life matter": Mandel, "Full of Life Now," p. 64.
    "[T]o a discerning eye": Quoted in Carlisle, *Loren Eiseley*, p. 186.

II Memory and Myth

20. "an autobiography does not: Fleischman, *Figures*, p. 13.
    "a network of intelligibility": Quoted by Charmé, *Meaning and Myth*, p. 17. Charmé and Serge Videman (whose phrase it is) have the function of language in general in mind; I have made the application to the specific use of language by the autobiographer.
21. "A bit of the path": Kennan, *Memoirs*, p. 4.
26. In this way he describes: It should be noted that there is some inconsistency in Eiseley's handling of the origin of his insomnia. In *All the Strange Hours* he says the condition had "perhaps" started after Clyde's death, but he attributes its full onset to a fall that knocked him unconscious, an event that occurred several years later. "Some sort of interior thermostat had finally broken," he writes. "I could not sleep when I wanted" (*ASH*, 79). Yet this disparity does not diminish in any way the traumatic effect of his father's death upon the young Eiseley.
32. Once again we have to look: Eiseley's connection with Wimberly and his circle is fully presented by Christianson in Chapter 4, sections V and VI. His discussion of paleontological expeditions in which Eiseley participated takes up a portion of Chapter 6 and most of Chapter 7.
36. "Taken as referring": Campbell, *Myths to Live By*, p. 25.
38. "I know [it]": Muir, *Autobiography*, p. 45. Subsequent quotations in this paragraph of my text come from the same page of Muir's book.
39. "[C]onsider them both": Melville, *Moby-Dick*, p. 222.
40. "The natural inheritance": Quoted by José Donoso as the epigraph to *The Obscene Bird of Night*, n.p.

III Readings in the Book of Nature

42. "I lived these hours": The University of Pennsylvania Archives, Eiseley Papers, Box 20, File II.
43. "consubstantial with its author": Montaigne, *Complete Essays*, p. 504.
 "in autobiography the truth": Gusdorf, "Conditions and Limits," p. 43.
 "*Where am I?*": Heard, *Human Venture*, p. 16.
44. "an act of orientation": Gunn, *Autobiography*, p. 23.
45. "that experimentation with nature": Heard, p. 22.
 His complaint . . . Baconian type: It needs to be mentioned that Eiseley is not a denigrator of Bacon himself. On the contrary, in *The Man Who Saw Through Time* (1973) he celebrates Bacon's vision, his championing of an empirical approach to the study of nature. Eiseley of course recognizes the importance of what we now call the scientific method; what he deplores is the narrow, unrelenting application of that method in our century.
 "When you understand": Whitehead, *Science and the Modern World*, p. 199.
46. "naturalist autobiography": Elder, "John Muir," p. 375.
 "gifted Victorians": Angyal, *Loren Eiseley*, p. 37.
47. "No one reading Jeffers": Eiseley, "Foreword" to *Not Man Apart*, n.p.
 "the complete identification": Eiseley, "Music of the Mountain," p. 42.
50. "pent up in lath": Melville, *Moby-Dick*, p. 23. The following quotation in my text is from p. 24.
51. "It is now more": White, *Natural History*, p. 249.
52. "It scrapes out": White, p. 153. The following extended quotation is from p. 59.
53. "Looking straight up": Jefferies, *The Old House*, p. 34. The following brief quotation is from p. 35. The extended quotation in the next paragraph of my text is from p. 60.
54. "Let us not": Jefferies, *Jefferies' England*, p. 303. The subsequent quotations in this paragraph come from pp. 303–4, 124, and xvi.
55. "the spears of which": Hudson, *Naturalist in La Plata*, p. 6. The subsequent quotation in the paragraph is from p. 7. In the next paragraph the words "special moments" and "special grace" are from p. 8.
 "We may say": Hudson, *Book of a Naturalist*, pp. 210–11. The next quotation in the paragraph is from p. 211.
56. "Death is a reality": Hudson, *Afoot in England*, p. 256.
 "[T]he darkest imaginings": Hudson, *Land's End*, p. 222.
 "Though in many of its aspects": Melville, *Moby-Dick*, p. 163.
57. "a vast rebirth ritual": Hyman, "Henry Thoreau," p. 30.
57–58. "If I had the influence": Carson, *Sense of Wonder*, pp. 42–43.
58. "If the writer": White, *Natural History*, p. 14.
59. "can be achieved": Abrams, *Natural Supernaturalism*, p. 95.
 "Men esteem truth remote": Thoreau, *Walden*, p. 93.
60. "Innumerable little streams": Thoreau, p. 246. The subsequent quota-

tions from *Walden* in this and the next paragraph are from pp. 248 and 249.

63. "on a humble scale": Thoreau, *Walden*, p. 153. The subsequent quotations from *Walden* in this paragraph are (in order) from pp. 160, 165, 86, 162, 124, and 119.
    "is small in scale": Abrams, p. 98.
64. "is vast (hence suggestive . . .)": Abrams, p. 98.
65. "It was Matter": Thoreau, *Maine Woods*, pp. 70–71.
68. "Time is but the stream": Thoreau, *Walden*, p. 94.
72. As . . . Carlisle has . . . observed: Carlisle, *Loren Eiseley*, p. 167.

IV The Uses of Loneliness

74. He describes the latter: Eliade, *Sacred and Profane*, p. 13.
    His outlook is made evident: Freud, *Civilization*, p. 11. The two subsequent quotations in the paragraph are from pp. 19 and 12.
75. Eliade observes that: Eliade, p. 116.
    the *mysterium tremendum*: Otto's notion is referred to by Eliade, p. 9, and by Eiseley himself, *ST*, p. 189.
    "Religion," he writes: Tillich, "Loneliness and Solitude," p. 551.
77. "Painting is an act": Landau, "Loneliness and Creativity," p. 494.
78. Eiseley again reminds us: I have an anonymous publisher's reader to thank for calling my attention to the applicability of "Resolution and Independence" to Eiseley's presentation of his meetings with strangers.
    "numinous encounters": The phrase is W. H. Auden's and is used in his introduction to *ST*, p. 19.
83. "the starfish is a . . . monster": Caldwell, review of *UU*, p. 22.
    "the appearance of life": Eliade, p. 147.
91. "The solitude of the person": Eiseley Papers, University of Pennsylvania Archives, Box 25, File III.
    "The transcendent context": Novak, *Ascent of the Mountain*, p. xii.
    "recognizes a divine Reality": Huxley, *Perennial Philosophy*, p. iv.
93. "deeper than the deepest": Augustine, *Confessions*, p. 60.
    "the realm of the invisible": The phrase is Hannah Arendt's, and is quoted by Gunn, *Autobiography*, p. 37.
94. "the depth level": Gunn, p. 37, who again quotes Arendt.
    "we can experience": Progoff, *Well and Cathedral*, p. 162.
98. "a desire to reintegrate": Eliade, p. 91. The subsequent extended quotation is from p. 92.
101. "periodically finds his way": Eliade, p. 88.
102. "nostalgia for a situation": Eliade, p. 93.
    "Direct knowledge of the Ground": Huxley, p. 35.

V An Artist of Autumn

104. In *The Fall*: Camus, *The Fall*, p. 25.

105. "[M]an owes his . . . success": Carrington, *Guide*, p. 261.
"a common instinct": Carrington, p. 267.
107. "not to inform the reader": Spengemann, *Forms of Autobiography*, p. 113.
111. "a nothing that": Hemingway, *Short Stories*, p. 481. The next quoted phrase is from the same page.
111–12. "There were visions": Eiseley, "Autumn," p. 238. The next quotation in the paragraph is from p. 239.
115. one of his own poems: The poem is called "The Maya," and is contained in *AKA*, pp. 23–24.
117. "[N]o need of a story": Beckett, *Stories & Texts*, p. 93.
119. "to make a home": Kazin, "Self as History," p. 89.
"What we are": Jung, *Memories*, p. 3. The next quotation in the paragraph is from the same page.
120. "announces . . . an intention": Carlisle, *Loren Eiseley*, p. 151.

BIBLIOGRAPHY

The list below is restricted almost exlusively to those works, whether by Eiseley or other authors, that are explicitly referred to in my text.

WORKS BY LOREN EISELEY

Books

All the Night Wings. New York: Times Books, 1979.
All the Strange Hours. New York: Scribner's, 1975.
Another Kind of Autumn. New York: Scribner's, 1977.
The Firmament of Time. New York: Atheneum, 1960.
The Immense Journey. New York: Random House, 1957.
The Innocent Assassins. New York: Scribner's, 1973.
The Invisible Pyramid. New York: Scribner's, 1970.
The Night Country. New York: Scribner's, 1971.
The Star Thrower. New York: Times Books, 1978.
The Unexpected Universe. New York: Harcourt Brace Jovanovich, 1969.

Uncollected Prose Pieces

"Autumn—A Memory." *Prairie Schooner* 1 (Oct. 1927): 238–39.
"The Enchanted Glass." *American Scholar* 26 (Fall 1957): 478–92.
"Foreword" to *Not Man Apart: Lines from Robinson Jeffers*. Ed. David Brower. San Francisco: Sierra Club, 1965.
"Music of the Mountain." *Voices*, no. 67 (Dec.–Jan. 1932–33): 42–47.

WORKS BY OTHER AUTHORS

Abrams, M. H. *Natural Supernaturalism*. New York: Norton, 1971.

Adams, Henry. *The Education of Henry Adams*. Ed. Ernest Samuels. Boston: Houghton Mifflin, 1973.

Angyal, Andrew J. *Loren Eiseley*. Boston: Twayne Publishers, 1983.

Anon. *Beowulf*. Tr. Burton Raffel. New York: New American Library, 1963.

Anon. "The Wanderer." In *Poems from the Old English*. 2nd ed. Tr. Burton Raffel. Lincoln: University of Nebraska Press, 1964.

Auden, W. H. *The Dyer's Hand and Other Essays*. New York: Random House, 1962.

———. "Introduction" to *The Star Thrower*. New York: Times Books,1978.

Augustine. *The Confessions of Saint Augustine*. Tr. Rex Warner. New York: New American Library, 1963.

Baker, Russell. "Life with Mother." In *Inventing the Truth: The Art and Craft of Memoir*. Ed. William Zinsser. Boston: Houghton Mifflin, 1987.

Beckett, Samuel. *Stories & Texts for Nothing*. New York: Grove Press,1967.

The Best American Essays, 1986. Ed. Elizabeth Hardwick. Series editor, Robert Atwan. New York: Ticknor & Fields, 1986.

The Best American Essays, 1988. Ed. Annie Dillard. Series editor, Robert Atwan. New York: Ticknor & Fields, 1988.

Broun, Heywood Hale. Interview with Loren Eiseley concerning *All the Strange Hours*. New York: Jeffrey Norton Publishers, Cassette #40128, 1975.

Caldwell, William A. Review of *The Unexpected Universe* in *The Sunday Record Call*. Nov. 23, 1969, p. 22.

Campbell, Joseph. *Myths to Live By*. New York: Bantam Books, 1973.

Camus, Albert. *The Fall*. Tr. Justin O'Brien. New York: Random House, 1956.

Carlisle, E. Fred. *Loren Eiseley: The Development of a Writer*. Urbana: University of Illinois Press, 1983.

Carrington, Richard. *A Guide to Earth History*. New York: New American Library, 1961.

Carson, Rachel. *The Sense of Wonder*. New York: Harper & Row, 1965.

Charmé, Stuart L. *Meaning and Myth in the Study of Lives: A Sartrean Perspective*. Philadelphia: University of Pennsylvania Press, 1984.

Chopin, Kate. *The Awakening and Selected Stories*. Ed. Sandra M. Gilbert. New York: Penguin Books, 1964.

Christianson, Gale E. *Fox at the Wood's Edge: A Biography of Loren Eiseley*. New York: Henry Holt & Co., 1990.

Cooke, Michael G. "The Hero in Autobiography." *Yale Review* 65 (Autumn 1975–Summer 1976): 587–93.

Donoso, José. *The Obscene Bird of Night*. Tr. Hardie St. Martin and Leonard Mades. New York: Alfred A. Knopf, 1973.

Edel, Leon. "The Mystery of Walden Pond." In *Stuff of Sleep and Dreams*. New York: Harper & Row, 1982.

Elder, John C. "John Muir and the Literature of Wilderness." *Massachusetts Review* 22 (Summer 1981): 375–86.
Eliade, Mircea. *The Sacred and the Profane*. New York: Harcourt, Brace & World, 1959.
Fleishman, Avrom. *Figures of Autobiography*. Berkeley: University of California Press, 1983.
Forster, E. M. *Two Cheers for Democracy*. New York: Harcourt, Brace and Company, 1951.
Freud, Sigmund. *Civilization and Its Discontents*. New York: Norton, 1962.
Gerber, Leslie E., and Margaret McFadden. *Loren Eiseley*. New York: Frederick Ungar, 1983.
Gunn, Janet Varner. *Autobiography: Toward a Poetics of Experience*. Philadelphia: University of Pennsylvania Press, 1982.
Gusdorf, Georges. "The Conditions and Limits of Autobiography." In *Autobiography: Essays Theoretical and Critical*. Ed. James Olney. Princeton, N.J.: Princeton University Press, 1980.
Heard, Gerald. *The Human Venture*. New York: Harper and Brothers, 1955.
Hemingway, Ernest. "A Clean, Well-Lighted Place." In *The Short Stories of Ernest Hemingway*. New York: Modern Library, 1942.
Hochfield, George. *Henry Adams: An Introduction and Interpretation*. New York: Barnes & Noble, 1962.
Holmes, Richard. *Footsteps: Adventures of a Romantic Biographer*. New York: Penguin Books, 1986.
Homer. *The Odyssey*. Tr. Robert Fitzgerald. Garden City, N.Y.: Doubleday (Anchor), 1963.
Hudson, W. H. *Afoot in England*. London: J. M. Dent & Sons, 1923.
———. *The Book of a Naturalist*. London: J. M. Dent & Sons, 1923.
———. *Land's End*. London: J. M. Dent & Sons, 1923.
———. *The Naturalist in La Plata*. London: J. M. Dent & Sons, 1923.
Huxley, Aldous. *The Perennial Philosophy*. Cleveland: World Publishing Company, 1962.
Hyman, Stanley Edgar. "Henry Thoreau in Our Times." In *The Promised End*. Cleveland: World Publishing Company, 1963.
Jefferies, Richard. *Jefferies' England: Nature Essays by Richard Jefferies*. Ed. Samuel J. Looker. London: Constable and Company,1937.
———. *The Old House at Coate*. Ed. Samuel J. Looker. Cambridge: Harvard University Press, 1948.
Jung, C. G. *Memories, Dreams, Reflections*. Rev. ed. New York: Pantheon Books, 1973.
Kazin, Alfred. "The Self as History: Reflections on Autobiography." In *Telling Lives*. Ed. Marc Pachter. Washington, D.C.: New Republic Books, 1979.
Kennan, George F. *Memoirs: 1925–1950*. Boston: Little, Brown, 1967.
Landau, Jacob. "Loneliness and Creativity." In *The Anatomy of Loneliness*. Ed. Joseph Hartog, J. Ralph Audy, and Yehudi A. Cohen. New York: International Universities Press, 1980.

Mandel, Barrett J. "Full of Life Now." In *Autobiography: Essays Theoretical and Critical*. Ed. James Olney. Princeton, N.J.: Princeton University Press, 1980.

Melville, Herman. *Moby-Dick*. Ed. Alfred Kazin. Boston: Houghton Mifflin, 1956.

Montaigne, Michel de. *The Complete Essays of Montaigne*. Tr. Donald Frame. Stanford, Calif.: Stanford University Press, 1958.

Muir, Edwin. *An Autobiography*. New York: William Sloane, 1954.

Novak, Michael. *Ascent of the Mountain, Flight of the Dove*. New York: Harper & Row, 1971.

Pascal, Roy. *Design and Truth in Autobiography*. Cambridge: Harvard University Press, 1960.

Progoff, Ira. *The Well and the Cathedral*. 2nd ed. New York: Dialogue House Library, 1977.

Schwartz, James M. "Loren Eiseley: The Scientist as Literary Artist." *Georgia Review* 31 (Winter 1977): 855–71.

Spengemann, William C. *The Forms of Autobiography*. New Haven, Conn.: Yale University Press, 1980.

Thoreau, Henry D. *The Maine Woods*. Ed. Joseph J. Moldenhauer. Princeton, N.J.: Princeton University Press, 1972.

———. *The Variorum Walden*. Ed. Walter Harding. New York: Twayne Publishers, 1962.

———. "Walking." In *The Works of Thoreau*. Ed. Henry Seidel Canby. Boston: Houghton Mifflin, 1937.

Tillich, Paul. "Loneliness and Solitude." In *The Anatomy of Loneliness*. Ed. Joseph Hartog, J. Ralph Audy, and Yehudi A. Cohen. New York: International Universities Press, 1980.

van der Post, Laurens. *Patterns of Renewal*. Lebanon, Penn.: Pendle Hill Pamphlet #121, 1960.

White, Gilbert. *The Natural History of Selborne*. London: Oxford University Press, 1937.

Whitehead, Alfred North. *Science and the Modern World*. New York: Free Press, 1967.

Yeats, W. B. *The Collected Poems of W. B. Yeats*. New York: Macmillan, 1959.

Zinsser, William. "Nonfiction as the New American Literature." In *On Writing Well*. 3rd ed. New York: Harper & Row, 1985.

———. "Writing and Remembering." In *Inventing the Truth: The Art and Craft of Memoir*. Ed. William Zinsser. Boston: Houghton Mifflin, 1987.

INDEX